Unemployment and
labour market flexibility:
Spain

Unemployment and labour market flexibility: Spain

Juan Jimeno
and
Luis Toharia

INTERNATIONAL LABOUR OFFICE   GENEVA

Jimeno, J. F. and Toharia, Luis
Unemployment and labour market flexibility: Spain
Geneva, International Labour Office, 1994

/Labour flexibility/, /Labour market/, /Unemployment/, /Employment policy/, /Trend/, /Spain/. 13.01.2
ISBN 92-2-108741-7

ILO Cataloguing in Publication Data

Printed in Switzerland   VAU

Acknowledgements

We are grateful to many colleagues who, throughout the years, have discussed with us issues regarding Spanish labour markets. In particular, Samuel Bentolila and Juan J. Dolado commented on previous drafts of the chapters and provided very helpful comments. The original project of the book was to be carried out by Lluís Fina, who had to give it up when he joined the European Commission. Special thanks are due to him for allowing us to freely use the material he had started preparing for the book.

We are also grateful to the Spanish Ministry of Education for the research fellowship (BE90-287) granted to Luis Toharia, which allowed him to spend a short period in early 1991 at the Institute for Employment Research of the University of Warwick (United Kingdom), during which the project progressed substantially, and to discuss matters with Juan F. Jimeno, who was at the time Lecturer at the London School of Economics.

We also owe many thanks to Guy Standing and Loretta de Luca who were very patient with us through the long process of production of the book. The Book Publishing Section of the ILO provided professional editorial support and Ana Velarde and Carmen Arias (FEDEA) helped with the typing.

Of course, the responsibility for any errors and omissions lies solely with ourselves.

Contents

Page

Acknowledgements v

1. The Spanish experience 1

Introduction 1

The Francoist model of development: A frustrated modernization 2

The evolution of employment (1960-75) 6

Structural change, economic crisis and employment destruction (1975-85) . . . 8

The recovery of employment (1985-90) 15

Increased fixed-term employment 18

The persistence of unemployment 20

Unemployment and labour market flexibility: Explaining the Spanish experience 21

2. The incidence of unemployment 25

Introduction 25

General overview 25

Labour force participation: Age and sex differentials 28

Unemployment: Characteristics of the unemployed 35

Regional disparities 41

The problem of first-job seekers 43

Long-term unemployment 43

The future prospects for unemployment 54

3. Wage flexibility 57

Introduction 57

Wage rigidity: Theoretical considerations and the relationship between rigidity
and the equilibrium rate of unemployment 59

Unemployment-inflation trade-offs and the equilibrium unemployment rate . . 60

The determinants of wage rigidity 63

A. Capital accumulation and the unemployment rate 63

B. Mismatch between labour supply and labour demand 64

C. Labour mobility 64

D. The composition of unemployment by duration 65

    E. Collective bargaining and the role of the unions   66
    F. Specific factors affecting the evolution of the Spanish NAIRU   66
  Wages and the employment crisis (1975-85)   67
  The influence of incomes policies   74
  Empirical evidence on wage rigidity and some estimations of the equilibrium
    rate of unemployment   78
  Collective bargaining: The legal framework   80
    "Rules of the game"   80
    Minimum wage laws   83
    Working hours restrictions   84
    The characteristics of collective bargaining and wage flexibility   84
  Concluding remarks   88

4. Employment flexibility   91

  Introduction   91
  ✳The "rigidity" of the Francoist labour market and the employment crisis
    (1975-85)   92
  The regulation of employment contracts and firings   94
  The incidence of fixed-term employment   96
  Firings costs and job creation   104
  Employment adjustment costs in Spain   107
  Other effects of fixed-term employment contracts   109
  ✦ Concluding remarks   110

✤ *5. Unemployment and labour market policy: Past, present and future*   113

  Introduction   113
  The reform of employment contracts as an employment promotion policy . . .   115
  Employment subsidies, public employment and work-sharing   116
  ✳The unemployment protection system   120
  ✦Policies aimed at reducing mismatch   125
  ✦Concluding remarks   128

References   131

Appendix
  Logit models of the probability of escaping unemployment into employment
    between 1988 and 1990, by gender   137

Tables:

1. Annual average growth rates of output and employment by broad sectors,
   Spain, 1960-75 (percentages)   6
2. Share of broad economic sectors in civilian employment, various OECD
   regions and countries, 1960-85 (percentages)   7
3. Annual average growth rates of output and employment by broad sectors,
   Spain, 1975-85   11
4. Government employment, various OECD regions and countries, 1973-87 . . .   13

5. Evolution of employment, by work status, Spain, 1976-90   13
6. Evolution of employment by broad occupational groups, Spain, 1976-90 . .   14
7. Annual average growth rates of output and employment by broad sectors,
   Spain, 1985-90 (percentages).   15
8. Percentage of fixed-term workers according to the *Labour Force Survey* and
   the Bank of Spain survey, by main industrial sectors   19
9. Number of permanent and fixed-term, full-time and part-time employees,
   Spain, 1987-90 (second quarter) . . . . :   20
10. Labour force, employment and unemployment by gender, Spain, 1977-91. .   21
11. Standardized unemployment rates in selected OECD countries, 1974-89 . .   28
12. Male and female participation rates with respect to population aged 15 years
    and over and aged 15-64, Spain, 1964-89   29
13. Participation rates by gender in 15 selected OECD countries, 1974-89. . . .   29
14. Growth of the labour force in various OECD regions and countries, various
    periods, 1960-88 (average annual percentage).   34
15(a). Age characteristics of different groups of unemployed, Spain, 1987 and
       1990   37
15(b). Educational characteristics of different groups of unemployed, Spain,
       1987 and 1990   38
15(c). Family characteristics of different groups of unemployed, Spain, 1987
       and 1990   39
15(d). Job search characteristics of different groups of unemployed, Spain, 1987
       and 1990   40
15(e). Work experience characteristics of different groups of unemployed, Spain,
       1987 and 1990   41
16. Unemployment rates and employment-population ratios by region, Spain,
    1981-90   42
17. Long-term unemployment: Percentage of total unemployment and transition
    probabilities, Spain, 1987-91 (second quarter).   45
18(a). Age characteristics of the short- and long-term unemployed (STU, LTU)
       and the newly employed (NE), Spain, 1987 and 1990   48
18(b). Educational characteristics of the short- and long-term unemployed
       (STU, LTU) and the newly employed (NE), Spain, 1987 and 1990. . . .   49
18(c). Family characteristics of the short- and long-term unemployed (STU,
       LTU) and the newly employed (NE), Spain, 1987 and 1990   50
18(d). Job search characteristics of the short- and long term-unemployed (STU,
       LTU) and the newly employed (NE), Spain, 1987 and 1990.   51
18(e). Work experience characteristics of the short- and long-term unemployed
       (STU, LTU) and the newly employed (NE), Spain, 1987 and 1990 . . .   52
19. Estimates of required new job creation on different unemployment and
    labour force participation assumptions, in Spain, 1990-2000   54
20. Wage rate increases agreed in collective bargaining, and industry dispersion,
    Spain, 1983-89   74
21. Yearly earnings (thousands of pesetas), Spain, 1988   75
22. Economy-wide agreements and inflation in Spain, 1978-90   77
23. Nominal and real wage rigidity in OECD countries   79

24. Number of collective agreements, Spain, 1980-91.   81
25. Industrial distribution of collective agreements, Spain, 1983 and 1990. . . .   82
26. Number of collective agreements registered each month, Spain, average
    1985-90   85
27. Duration of collective agreements, Spain, 1988 and 1989.   87
28. Collective bargaining agreements containing special clauses, Spain, 1988. .   87
29. Incidence of fixed-term contracts by worker characteristics, Spain, 1987-90   97
30. Characteristics of fixed-term and permanent workers, by gender, Spain,
    1987 and 1990.   100
31. Probability of achieving a permanent contract status for new jobholders,
    Spain, 1987 and 1990   102
32. Public expenditure on labour market programmes as a percentage of GDP
    in several OECD countries (average 1986-89).   114
33. Fixed-term employment contracts by type, Spain, 1984-89   116
34. Number of workers' cooperatives and their members, Spain, 1985-91   117
35. Workers affected by temporary lay-offs by broad sectors, Spain, 1979-91 . .   118
36. Workers who have capitalized their unemployment benefits to become
    self-employed, Spain, 1985-91   118
37. Components of labour costs (as a percentage of total costs) in manufacturing
    in some EC countries, 1988.   120
38. Duration of unemployment benefits in Spain, before and after the 1992
    reform   122
39. Evolution of expenses on unemployment benefits and their sources, Spain,
    1987-91 122
40. Unemployed persons per staff member in public employment services,
    selected European countries, 1988   126
41. "Job offers" registered with public employment agencies, Spain, 1978-91   126

Figures:

 1. The evolution of employment, labour force and unemployment in Spain,
    1970-90   2
 2. Comparison between the evolution of employment in Spain and the rest of
    OECD-Europe, 1970-89   9
 3. Employment-population ratios (population 15-64) in Spain compared with
    selected OECD countries, 1970-87.   10
 4. Evolution of employment by broad economic sectors, Spain, 1977-90. . . .   16
 5. Average yearly percentage change in employment by work status, 1976-85
    and 1987-90   17
 6. Percentage of employees with a fixed-term contract, Spain, 1987-91.   18
 7. Labour force participation rate and employment-population ratio, Spain,
    1970-90   26
 8. Unemployment rates in Spain, 1970-90: Standard, absolute and potentially
    observed if labour force participation rate had remained at its 1974 level . .   27
 9. Male age-specific labour force participation rates, 1964-89.   30
10. Female age-specific labour force participation rates, 1964-89   31

11. Distribution of life situations of young males, 15(16)-19 and 20-24, Spain, 1964-89   32

12. Distribution of life situations of young females, 15(16)-19 and 20-24, Spain, 1964-89   33

13. Distribution of life situations of older people aged 50-64, by gender, Spain, 1964-89   34

14. Standard male unemployment rates by age, 1964-89   35

15. Standard female unemployment rates by age, 1964-89   36

16. Proportion of unemployed aged 16-24 with and without past job experience, Spain, 1976-90   44

17. "Survival probabilities" of unemployed males after 1 year (LTU) and 2 years (VLTU), Spain, 1977-90   46

18. "Survival probabilities" of unemployed females after 1 year (LTU) and 2 years (VLTU), Spain, 1977-90   46

19. Unemployment rates and proportion of long-term unemployment, by regions (Autonomous Communities), Spain, 1991 (second quarter)   47

20. Probabilities of "escaping" unemployment into employment, males and females, Spain, 1989-90.   53

21. An illustrative example of the neoclassical concept of labour market flexibility   59

22. The equilibrium unemployment rate: (1) wage equation, (2) price equation .   61

23. Unemployment and inflation in Spain and the EC, 1970-89   62

24. Wage increases in manufacturing in Spain and other western countries, 1978-85   68

25. Evolution of wage share in GDP, unadjusted and adjusted for the changing proportion of wage and salary earners, Spain, 1970-84   69

26. Non-wage labour costs as a proportion of total employee compensation, Spain, 1970-84   70

27. Evolution of real wages and unit labour costs, Spain, 1970-87   71

28. Wage differentials by industry and occupation, Spain, 1965-87   72

29. *Ex ante* expected profits from hiring a worker   106

30. A "high unemployment trap"   107

31. Percentage of unemployed people covered by the unemployment protection system, Spain, 1976-89   123

Chapter 1

The Spanish experience

Spain has suffered from the same problem as most European countries, but in a stronger form. The specificity comes from the Franco legacy, which left Spain in the mid-70s with both an archaic system of labour relations and an inadequate production structure. (Bentolila and Blanchard, 1990, p. 233.)

Introduction

The Spanish economy has undergone a complete transformation during the last two decades. The labour market has been one of the areas where this transformation has been most traumatic. The old autocratic economic system was bound to be reformed eventually, but unfortunately this change and political reform coincided with the economic crisis of the mid-1970s and early 1980s. This coincidence deepened the economic crisis, sending unemployment to levels way beyond those reached in other Western European and OECD countries, peaking at 21.6 per cent in 1985. The recovery that started in 1985, despite generating very strong employment growth, has not been able to reduce unemployment significantly. A new system of economic relations had to be put in place during these troubled years. Many inefficiencies inherited from the old system persisted, while supporters of complete liberalization of the labour market and those of re-regulating it were engaged in a heated debate. Even now, a decade and a half after the advent of democracy and along the path to European Monetary Union (EMU, hereafter), the design of a "Spanish model" of economic relations is not fully clear. For this reason, we think that it is more appropriate to begin this book by referring to the "Spanish experience" rather than to that non-existent "Spanish model".

Figure 1 summarizes broadly the recent labour market developments in Spain by showing the evolution of the labour force and employment, and hence unemployment, in the two decades to 1990. There have been quite dramatic shifts in employment in the last 25 years or so. It grew slowly but steadily during the years of economic expansion of the 1960s and early 1970s, the golden days of economic development under the Franco regime. The international economic crisis following the first oil shock in 1973 was felt in Spain with some delay, but employment stabilized in 1975 and started a sharp decline in 1977. Contrary to what happened in other Western countries, it was this fall in employment, rather than the failure to create jobs and labour supply factors, which was the main cause of the huge rise in unemployment. Employment continued to drop until mid-1985, after which it rose again at an unprecedented rate. However, this employment recovery also set in motion unprecedented increases in labour force participation rates (especially among women), so that there was only a minor reduction in unemployment (down to about 16 per cent by 1990). As we shall see, the dramatic shifts in employment have been accompanied by important changes in the structure of employment.

Figure 1.   The evolution of employment, labour force and unemployment in Spain, 1970-90

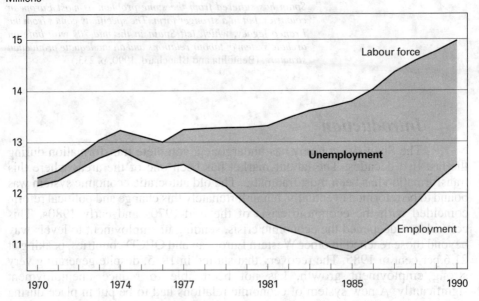

Millions

This chapter describes the three main elements of the Spanish experience, namely the employment crisis of 1975-85, the post-1985 economic and employment recovery and the persistence of unemployment despite the favourable evolution of employment. These are the contexts to which our discussion of labour market flexibility will be related in later chapters. In order to understand this evolution properly, however, it is necessary to begin with a brief description of the economic system of the Franco regime and the results of that system during the 1960s and early 1970s.

The Francoist model of development: A frustrated modernization[1]

Partly for ideological reasons and partly out of necessity, a principal economic policy objective of the Franco years was self-sufficiency. However, this autarkic model failed when it proved impossible to construct a totally self-reliant economy. Traditional exports of agricultural products were insufficient to finance essential imports and this, together with strong internal inflationary pressures, was the main cause of a serious foreign exchange crisis at the end of the 1950s. Then, the Government was obliged to request the aid of the IMF and other international agencies, and to agree to their recommendations. These consisted largely of measures designed to clean up the financial mess in the public sector, establish a realistic exchange rate and lift various barriers to internal and external trade. As it turned out, this was just what was needed to permit the Spanish economy to take advantage of the economic boom that had begun elsewhere in the Western world a few years earlier. However, in spite of the abandonment of the autarkic model, the economy continued to be propelled largely by the domestic market, in particular by demand stimulated by the wage increases which large firms began to grant as a result of the collective bargaining system introduced in 1958. Furthermore, the external constraints on economic growth were considerably relaxed with the appearance of three new sources of financial inflows such as foreign exchange brought by the first influx of tourists from abroad, foreign investment for which conditions had been made easier by the 1959 reforms, and remittances home by the huge number of Spanish migrants working elsewhere in Europe. After these reforms, the strategy for the development of the Spanish economy pursued until the early 1970s was based on:

   (i)   fast-growing domestic demand,

   (ii) abundant reserves of inexpensive labour,

   (iii) the power of employers to control the labour force by suppressing its most basic rights,

   (iv) the subordination of the public sector and the social welfare system to private interests,

   (v) a sectoral distribution of production concentrated on a few sectors (construction, primary and fabricated metal, transport equipment), which turned out to be the sectors worst hit by the international crisis of the mid-1970s and early 1980s, and

   (vi) protection of domestic firms against foreign competition.

At the beginning of the 1970s, it was already evident that this strategy was doomed. The capacity of the domestic market was relatively limited and did not allow businesses to specialize to the extent that would have enabled them to profit from economies of scale, using their (largely imported) equipment to full capacity. Access to foreign markets was severely restricted, often because Spanish firms were operating under licences from foreign companies which explicitly prohibited exporting. In other cases, Spanish firms were unable to take their products abroad simply because they were copies of foreign products or models, or because the lack of an indigenous technology prevented them from being competitive for non-price reasons.

High trade barriers shielded Spanish firms from foreign competition, so that during the period of rapid growth the most modern firms were able to prosper even though they were not specialized and their equipment was not used to its fullest capacity. Relatively high production costs and prices enabled numerous tiny firms to survive on very little capital. Extreme fragmentation was thus a characteristic of Spanish manufacturing in the Franco years. There was a plethora of small businesses and factories that differed from their counterparts in more industrialized countries in their lack of innovation and their low technological level (Donges, 1984).

The growth of Spanish firms was also limited by the shortage of skilled labour. In other cases, the lack of skilled labour made it impossible to increase production of some specific product lines and, to a great extent, this shortage explains the low levels of productivity in most Spanish firms during this period. In many cases, this lack of skills extended even to company owners and managers. Over the years a generation of "new entrepreneurs" had emerged, former skilled workers or owners of small manufacturing firms whose years of experience had given them a certain technological background, and who were skilled at identifying market segments where unfulfilled demand existed. However, as shown in a series of case studies collected by González of medium-sized manufacturers of durable consumer goods, these people were not familiar with management techniques or the tools of economic planning and project evaluation (González, 1985). Furthermore, they tended to be suspicious of any knowledge acquired outside the firm itself and underrated the importance of the organizational aspects of business. This led them to commit errors, to start product lines that were doomed to fail from the outset, and to multiply production inefficiencies. Whatever use of management techniques they made was limited to mere formalities, adopted more because techniques were fashionable than because they were useful tools that would yield profits.

The public sector's reaction to these shortcomings amounted to little more than rhetoric. Analysts all agree that measures adopted by the public sector in an attempt to promote home-grown technology were utterly insufficient. What little was done was uncoordinated and unstable (Martín and Rodríguez, 1977; Molero, 1983). As an example, in 1974 the average EEC investment in research and development was 1.5 per cent of GNP, but only 0.31 per cent in Spain. Things were not much different in the field of education, although social pressures forced the authorities gradually to increase their provision. However, their actions were limited to a passive acceptance of society's demands and the establishment of a simple *à la carte* variety of vocational training schemes aimed at making it easier for unskilled workers from rural areas to adapt to new jobs in industry. According to OECD estimates, only 1.8 per cent of GNP was allocated to education in Spain, as opposed to between 4.5 per cent and 8 per cent in leading European countries (OECD, 1986b).

Two other company traits of this period should be mentioned because of their important role in making it particularly difficult for Spanish firms to weather the economic crisis and the political changes of the mid-1970s. These were their unbalanced financial structure and their attitudes towards labour relations. This last factor created numerous grievances, which were aggravated by some more general developments, leading to an accumulation of unmet claims.

Financial experts agree that Spanish businesses suffered from a comparatively low level of self-financing and an excessive amount of short-term debt (Cuervo, 1986). To this, one could add the common recourse to "irregular" practices, of which the confusion between personal and business assets is a good example, although perhaps not the most scandalous. According to González (1985), failure to define the limits of a particular business often led firms to commit their resources to odd, highly risky activities which, in many cases, triggered or aggravated a crisis. Furthermore, many firms financed their rapid expansion with the help of transfers and special credits at subsidized rates and with other assistance provided by the public sector.

Regarding labour relations, the few available studies on the subject all agree that these oscillated between extreme authoritarianism and paternalism, except for a few companies that were modern or had largely foreign capital, which preferred to face labour issues openly through direct negotiations with their employees and bypass the Francoist institutions (Amsden, 1972). In many other large enterprises, particularly in the public sector, authoritarianism was common practice. Tight political controls were exercised, sometimes with the direct collaboration of the state police. This situation continued until well into the 1970s and is documented in cases such as RENFE (the Spanish railways) and SEAT (automobiles) (Ferner, 1986; Miguélez, 1977). In the medium-sized firms studied by González (1985), most employers felt that labour relations should take care of themselves. Personnel management was limited to clerical matters and any problems that might arise, no matter how minor, were generally a signal for the personal intervention of the employer himself. These practices remained unchanged even as businesses grew and the traditional channels of communication broke down. According to González, conflicts began to multiply and the personal intervention of employers was not always consistent. The gap between management and labour continued to widen and numerous complaints accumulated, with no apparent channels for solving them.

Other, more general, complaints stemmed from the very nature of the Francoist labour organization and the peculiar system of collective bargaining established in 1958. This latter system, which permitted employees a certain amount of representation in medium and large firms, and the existence of genuine collective bargaining practices (always provided that the employer was willing to accept them), contributed to the creation of different forms of labour organization. These organizations pressed not only for higher wages and better working conditions, but also for freedom to organize and the re-establishment of democracy. The system also produced a dichotomy between the wages and working conditions of employees able to exert a direct influence on their companies, and those who were unable to organize and were obliged to leave such matters to the Francoist labour organization. In fact, during the boom years, wage differentials by industries became larger rather than smaller, as might have been expected (Badosa, 1979). The most traditional sectors, composed mainly of small firms where wages were lower and production more fragmented, gradually slipped further behind.

Another important source of cumulative grievances was the growing fiscal burden on wages and salaries. In the mid-1960s, manual workers' wages lost their long-standing exemption from direct taxation. At the same time, a "family bonus" instituted in the mid-1940s to keep married women out of the labour market which had become fairly large, was frozen in order to achieve the opposite effect in a tighter labour market. As a result, the ratio of net to gross wages rapidly deteriorated. For example, for a typical unskilled manual worker, this ratio dropped from 1.08 in 1967 to 0.93 in 1975 (Fina, 1983). Moreover, all these changes took place within a fiscal system that was extremely regressive, not only by design, but more particularly, because of the widespread tax evasion practised by the rich.

The evolution of employment (1960-75)

Despite all these weaknesses, in the early 1960s the Spanish economy embarked upon a phase of sustained economic growth. The average increase in GDP in this decade was about 7 per cent per annum, which permitted Spain to recover, to some extent, the position lost in the preceding quarter of a century. Employment also increased, but only modestly, since very high increases in productivity during this period meant that production could rise rapidly without creating many new jobs. Unemployment rates were kept low by the flow of emigrants towards other European countries and by low participation rates (especially among women). As table 1 shows, employment increased throughout the 1960s at a annual rate of 0.6 per cent, which compares with the average growth of real GDP of more than 7.5 per cent, and natural population growth of 1.2 per cent. Employment growth increased somewhat in the early 1970s, at a time when GDP growth slowed down.

Table 1. *Annual average growth rates of output and employment by broad sectors, Spain, 1960-75 (percentages)*

	1960-65	1965-70	1970-75
Real GDP (at 1970 market prices)			
Agriculture	1.1	2.1	4.2
Non-agrarian	10.5	6.8	4.3
Manufacturing	12.0	9.1	6.7
Construction	15.0	6.9	3.0
Services	8.6	6.0	5.2
Total	8.6	6.2	4.3
Employment			
Agriculture	−3.1	−2.6	−4.4
Non-agrarian	3.1	2.1	2.8
Manufacturing	1.6	1.6	2.5
Construction	4.2	2.8	1.1
Services	3.9	2.4	3.5
Total	0.6	0.6	0.8

Source: *Labour Force Survey* and *National Accounts*.

However, although aggregate employment did not rise by much, the structure of employment changed dramatically. Employment tumbled in agriculture between 1960 and 1975; agriculture's share in the total labour force fell from around 40 per cent to just over 20 per cent, a drop of almost 20 percentage points

Table 2. **Share of broad economic sectors in civilian employment, various OECD regions and**
            countries, 1960-85 (percentages)

	1960	1970	1975	1980	1985
Agriculture					
OECD	21.6	13.8	11.6	10.0	8.7
EC	21.1	11.5	9.5	8.2	8.6
Spain	38.7	26.9	21.9	18.9	18.2
Germany (Fed. Rep.)	14.0	8.6	7.4	6.0	5.4
France	22.5	13.9	10.2	8.8	7.6
Italy	32.6	20.2	16.7	14.2	11.2
United Kingdom	4.7	3.2	2.7	2.7	2.5
Industry (including construction)					
OECD	35.3	36.9	35.0	33.7	31.0
EC	39.8	42.5	40.3	38.3	33.6
Spain	30.3	35.6	38.4	36.1	31.9
Germany (Fed. Rep.)	47.0	48.5	46.0	44.8	41.0
France	37.6	39.7	38.7	35.9	32.0
Italy	33.9	39.5	39.1	37.8	33.6
United Kingdom	47.7	44.8	40.7	38.1	31.6
Services					
OECD	43.1	49.2	53.5	56.3	60.2
EC	39.1	45.9	50.2	53.5	57.7
Spain	31.0	37.5	39.8	45.1	49.9
Germany (Fed. Rep.)	39.1	42.9	46.6	49.2	53.5
France	39.9	46.4	51.1	55.3	60.4
Italy	33.5	40.3	44.2	48.0	55.2
United Kingdom	47.6	52.0	56.6	59.2	65.9

Source: OECD, *Historical Statistics*, Paris, various years.

in only 15 years (see table 2, which compares the change in Spain to that of other
EC and OECD countries). The rural population quickly dwindled and aged, while
industrial cities and their immediate surroundings continued the rapid growth
initiated in the second half of the preceding decade (García-Barbancho, 1975, pp.
53-61). The drop in agricultural employment was more than made up by the
increase in employment in the other major sectors. Throughout the period, the
service sector was the most dynamic, both in relative and absolute terms. The
service industry that grew most was "professional services" (including banks,
insurance companies and business services), as is to be expected in a period of
strong economic growth. Even some more traditional services such as retailing and
transport also experienced significant growth, though some soon began showing
signs of saturation. The growth of employment in the service sector slowed in the
second half of the decade, only to pick up again at the beginning of the 1970s, as
the demand for collective services in the fields of education and health gained
momentum. In contrast to the situation prevailing a decade earlier, the public sector

began contributing actively to employment growth in the service sector (Fina and Wilson, 1984).

The construction industry did a good deal to generate employment. Furthermore, it served as a "bridge" for immigrants from the countryside to the industrial cities or to other parts of Europe. The boom in construction was triggered by three exceptional circumstances. First, large-scale population movements within the country gave rise to a great demand for housing. Second, increases in purchasing power activated the housing market, which had been extremely sluggish since the mid-1950s. Finally, tourism created additional demand. However, the growth of employment in the construction sector began to slow in the late 1960s and, even more, in the early 1970s. Purely cyclical factors alone were not to blame for this. The exceptional increase in demand mentioned above was coming to an end, a process which became more acute as the influx of manpower from the agricultural sector began to wane. Additionally, the construction sector was beginning to introduce certain technological innovations.

The manufacturing sector also made a positive contribution to employment growth. Although its initial contribution was fairly moderate in relative terms, it became increasingly important as time went by and as the astonishing productivity gains of the early 1960s began to level off. Within manufacturing, durable consumer goods sectors and, above all, metal materials and transport equipment registered the greatest increases in employment. Employment also increased considerably in some of the basic industries which, with the help of generous state aid, embarked upon ambitious plans to increase capacity and cut down on imports. The share of industrial employment continued to grow in the early 1970s, when the other major industrial countries had already started a process of adjustment away from manufacturing (see table 2). Thus Spanish manufacturing became swollen at both ends (in basic and consumer goods) while production of intermediate goods products was seriously constricted (Segura, 1983). This composition of manufacturing employment was an important cause of the virulence of the employment crisis after 1975, as these sectors were especially hit by the international economic crisis.

Structural change, economic crisis and employment destruction (1975-85)

In the second half of the 1970s and in the early 1980s, the Spanish economy went through an employment crisis much more intense than that experienced in other OECD countries (figures 2 and 3). Civilian employment (as defined by the OECD) decreased at an average annual rate of 1.6 per cent. The employment-population ratio (total employment as a percentage of population 15-64 years old) was already one of the lowest among OECD countries in 1970, for reasons that we will discuss in Chapter 2 (only Italy, the Netherlands and Greece had lower employment-population ratios). This too experienced a substantial fall to 43.8 per cent in 1985, which was the lowest employment-population ratio in the OECD area.

Figure 2. **Comparison between the evolution of employment in Spain and the rest of OECD-Europe, 1970-89**

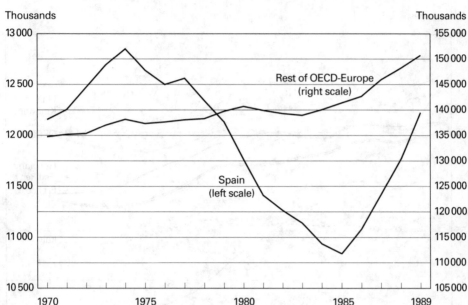

Table 3 shows the evolution of output and employment by broad economic sectors during the 1975-85 period. As this table shows, employment declined at an annual rate of more than 1.5 per cent for the whole period. For the first time, manufacturing and construction joined agriculture as sectors where employment was falling. Between 1975 and 1980, manufacturing jobs were lost at an annual rate of 2.5 per cent and construction jobs at a rate of 3.0 per cent. Between 1980 and 1985, these rates were even higher: 3.6 per cent in manufacturing and 5.5 per cent in construction.

Recalling the information contained in table 2 on the share of each broad economic sector in employment during this period for several OECD countries, we observe that the share of agricultural employment in Spain was among the highest in OECD countries, in both 1975 and 1985. Correspondingly, the share of employment in services was among the lowest. As elsewhere, the share of industry decreased, reaching levels similar to the OECD average. However, this process of deindustrialization occurred at a faster rate than that in other European countries, with the exception of the United Kingdom. As table 3 shows, there were big falls in agricultural employment between 1975 and 1985, especially in the first part of the period, which continued the accelerating decline of the 1960s and early 1970s. Given the drastic drop in employment opportunities in the rest of the economy, this might seem surprising. Perhaps, faced with the prospect of stiffer competition once within the EC, Spanish agriculture, which provided (and still provides) a substantial proportion of total employment, began speeding up the process of modernization.

Two other factors led to employment losses in agriculture. One was the ageing of rural population, as a consequence of the major exodus from the

Figure 3. *Employment-population ratios (population 15-64) in Spain compared with selected OECD countries, 1970-87*

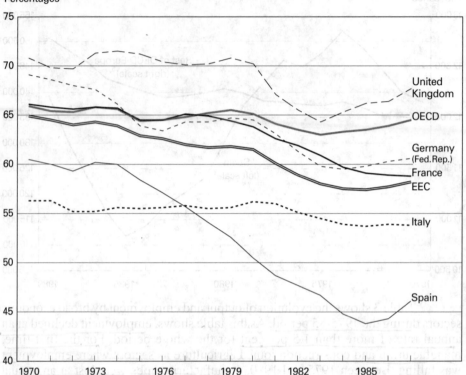

countryside during the two preceding decades. Another factor, which has not been sufficiently emphasized, is the increase in social security and welfare coverage which occurred in the early 1970s. The number of pensions paid to agricultural workers increased by some 250,000 between 1975 and 1980.[2] It is very likely that a high proportion of these pensioners simply began collecting pensions, without any change in their usual way of life (apart from their own perception of no longer belonging to the labour force). This may also have contributed to the fact that, although agricultural employment fell drastically, the rural population increased considerably between 1975 and 1980 rather than registering losses as before.[3]

This partly fictitious drop in employment may have also occurred in the manufacturing and service sectors. The increase in social security benefits could explain the sharp decline in the number of small businessmen and self-employed manufacturing workers which was observed in the early years of the crisis, particularly in such traditional sectors as the textile, garment and wood industries (Jaumandreu, 1986). It could also partly explain the drop in employment in some service branches such as retailing, transport or personal services, and the slow growth of others, which will be examined later. One should keep in mind that, in terms of the national accounts, social welfare expenditure rose from barely 7 per

Table 3. *Annual average growth rates of output and employment by broad sectors, Spain, 1975-85*

	1975-80	1980-85
Real GDP (at 1980 market prices)		
Agriculture	1.7	1.0
Non-agrarian	1.8	1.4
Manufacturing	2.0	0.7
Construction	-3.1	-0.3
Services	2.6	3.3
Total	1.8	1.4
Employment		
Agriculture	-6.2	-2.7
Non-agrarian	-0.6	-1.4
Manufacturing	-2.5	-3.6
Construction	-3.0	-5.5
Services	1.3	0.6
Total	-1.8	-1.6

Source: *Labour Force Survey* and *National Accounts.*

cent of GDP in 1970 to almost 15 per cent in 1984. Its composition also shifted towards a higher proportion of social security subsidies.

The number of jobs in manufacturing declined in almost all industries, although to a varying degree. Traditional industries, such as machinery, electrical equipment and textiles, were the hardest hit, due to both the segmentation of demand and increases in productivity. At the same time, job losses were substantial in industries like metals and transport equipment, which grew particularly fast during the boom years of the preceding decade. In fact, during these boom years, the Spanish economy had become specialized in precisely those industries that were hardest hit by the economic crisis in Spain and elsewhere (Martínez et al., 1982).

The decline in manufacturing jobs in Spain differed from that in most other European countries, in that Spanish job losses went hand in hand with a significant increase in labour productivity. As can be computed from the figures in table 3, manufacturing productivity increased at an average annual rate of 4.5 per cent between 1975 and 1980 and 4.4 per cent between 1980 and 1985, thus implying a global improvement over the whole decade of about 56 per cent. Moreover, as table 3 shows, there was some growth of output during this period. Thus the large increase in productivity was not due solely to the statistical effect of the demise of the least efficient units because, in this extreme case, production would have fallen.

In fact, productivity increased more in those organizations that were initially more productive than in their more inefficient counterparts. As a result, production became increasingly concentrated among a limited number of firms: while in 1973 the 500 leading Spanish manufacturing firms accounted for 38.8 per cent of all production, this figure was 51.3 per cent in 1981. However, their share of total employment rose only from 29.7 per cent to 31.6 per cent (Jaumandreu, 1986). There is also abundant evidence that manufacturing firms made record gains in productivity very rapidly, sometimes even without having to make large investments in machinery and equipment. Many of these firms simply altered their systems of organization and improved their management methods, sometimes thanks to the arrival of a new foreign partner. On other occasions, whole industries, particularly those being "officially restructured", were reshuffled with the help of generous state aid. Productive activity was reorganized and modernized, while mergers of firms were fostered in order to achieve a higher degree of specialization.

The construction industry also experienced a sharp decline in employment. This decline was closely linked to the fall in production (see table 3), which in turn stemmed from the drop in demand. The latter had various causes and, as already mentioned, not all were directly related to the economic crisis. The following factors exerted negative influences on the construction industry:

(i)   A big decrease in internal migration and the stagnation or decline in the population of big cities, to which manpower used to migrate.

(ii)   A sharp decline in marriage rates, which began in 1976 and became more pronounced after 1980 (Fernández Cordón, 1986).

(iii) Stagnation of the growth in demand for residential construction in tourist zones, many of which had reached saturation point.

(iv)   Stricter urban planning controls as a result of the democratic election of local governments.

(v)   The decline in private investment.

(vi)   The decline, or at least the stagnation, of public investment during most of this period. This was either due to more rigorous planning and evaluation of investment projects, or to the fact that it was politically more expedient to reject investments than to resist social pressures to increase spending in other areas, at a time when deficits were high and still rising and when it was difficult to raise public revenues.

Throughout the period under consideration, the service sector generally made a positive, though modest and declining, contribution to the growth in employment. Important declines were registered in some of the more traditional service industries: retailing, transport and personal services, particularly domestic services. Other service industries grew more strongly. Outstanding among them, as in other countries, were business services, where public employment played a leading role. According to the labour force survey, employment in "education and research" grew at an average annual rate of 3.5 per cent between 1977 and 1985, and employment in public administration at a rate of 2.9 per cent. Overall, public sector employment (including state-owned manufacturing firms) increased at an average annual rate of 3.8 per cent.[4] This is undoubtedly one of the most salient traits of this period, and it is clearly linked to the new political circumstances (Fina and Wilson, 1984). However, despite these increases, the Spanish public sector continues to be comparatively small and employment in "social services" much more limited than in other European countries (see table 4).

Table 4.   Government employment, various OECD regions and countries, 1973-87

	% rates of growth		% total employment		
	1973-79	1979-87	1974	1980	1987
OECD	2.0	1.1	14.6	15.3	15.5
EC	2.2	1.2	15.1	16.9	18.2
Spain	–	3.2	9.3	11.9	13.3
Germany (Fed. Rep.)	2.2	1.0	13.2	14.9	16.1
France	–	2.0	–	20.0	23.2
United Kingdom	1.5	– 0.1	19.6	21.1	21.6
Italy	2.7	1.3	13.4	14.5	15.4

Source: OECD, *Historical Statistics*, 1989.

Table 5.   Evolution of employment, by work status, Spain, 1976-90

	Numbers				Average annual change			
	Thousands				Thousands		Percentages	
	IV-76	IV-85	II-87	II-90	1976-85	1987-90	1976-85	1987-90
Total employees	8 746.2	7 406.2	7 877.1	9 230.0	–148.9	451.0	–1.8	5.4
Private sector employees	7 404.2	5 530.4	6 091.6	7 152.5	–208.2	353.6	–3.2	5.5
Public sector employees	1 342.0	1 875.8	1 785.5	2 077.5	59.3	97.3	3.8	5.2
Total non-employees	3 726.8	3 184.2	3 410.3	3 295.1	–60.3	–38.4	–1.7	–1.1
Employers	414.4	333.1	398.2	470.8	–9.0	24.2	–2.4	5.7
Agricultural self-employed	1 138.0	847.1	797.5	706.8	–32.3	–30.2	–3.2	–3.9
Non-agricultural self-employed	1 084.6	1 242.7	1 454.2	1 441.2	17.6	–4.3	1.5	–0.3
Total self-employed	2 222.6	2 089.8	2 251.7	2 148.0	–14.8	–34.6	–0.7	–1.6
Family workers	1 089.8	761.3	760.4	676.3	–36.5	–28.0	–3.9	–3.8
Others	47.7	27.9	42.2	31.4	–	–	–	–
Grand total	12 520.7	10 618.3	11 329.6	12 556.5	–211.4	409.0	1.8	3.5

Source: Fernández, Garrido and Toharia (1991). The figures in the table correspond to the original data from the *Labour Force Survey*. Data between 1985 and 1987 are not strictly comparable because the methodological break on the series seriously affects the distribution by work status.

Tables 5 and 6 present data on the changes in the distribution of employment by work status and occupational group. They show that, over the ten years to 1985, the number of wage-earners in the private sector fell sharply while the number of non-agricultural self-employed and public sector employees increased. (This is a typical pattern in recessions which has reversed itself during the employment recovery in the second half of the 1980s, as it can be seen also from table 5.) On the other hand, a clear process of substitution of, broadly speaking, white-collar for blue-collar and agricultural occupations took place. While the latter experienced substantial job losses during the whole period of crisis, the former just about maintained employment in the first part and began gaining

Table 6. Evolution of employment by broad occupational groups, Spain, 1976-90

| | Numbers | | | | Average annual change | | | | | |
| | Thousands | | | | Thousands | | | Percentages | | |
	Q IV-76	Q IV-81	Q IV-85	Q IV-90	76-81	81-85	85-90	76-81	81-85	85-90
Professional and technical staff	745.4	761.1	940.6	1 403.6	3.1	44.9	92.6	0.4	5.4	8.3
Managers, etc.	195.2	179.8	186.0	240.1	-3.1	1.6	10.8	-1.6	0.9	5.2
Clerical workers	1 267.7	1 228.9	1 252.5	1 656.7	-7.8	5.9	80.8	-0.6	0.5	5.8
Sales and commercial workers	1 232.4	1 202.7	1 171.1	1 406.0	-5.9	-7.9	47.0	-0.5	-0.7	3.7
Service workers	1 409.1	1 434.5	1 551.9	1 717.6	5.1	29.4	33.1	0.4	2.0	2.0
Agricultural workers	2 713.6	2 036.0	1 832.2	1 407.0	-135.5	-50.9	-85.0	-5.6	-2.6	-5.1
Production non-agricultural workers	4 955.7	4 375.7	3 876.9	4 712.2	-116.0	-124.7	167.1	-2.5	-3.0	4.0
Not elsewhere classified	1.6	0.5	1.4	–	–	–	–	–	–	–
Armed forces	105.8	116.1	100.6	76.7	2.1	-3.9	-4.8	1.9	-3.5	-5.3
Total	12 626.7	11 331.2	10 911.0	12 408.3	-259.1	-105.1	299.5	-2.1	-0.9	2.6

Source: *Labour Force Survey*. The data for 1976, 1981 and 1985 have been modified to correct for the 1987 methodological break, which does not seriously affect the distribution by occupation. This explains why the total figures do not coincide with those of table 5.

Table 7. *Annual average growth rates of output and employment by broad sectors, Spain, 1985-90 (percentages)*

	1985	1986	1987	1988	1989	1990
Real GDP (at constant market prices) [1]						
Agriculture	3.1	−9.1	12.4	5.1	−6.9	2.8
Non-agrarian						
Manufacturing	2.1	5.6	4.4	4.4	3.4	1.6
Construction	2.2	5.9	8.3	10.9	13.7	10.4
Services	2.3	3.0	4.6	4.8	5.4	4.0
Total	2.3	3.3	5.6	5.2	4.8	3.7
Employment						
Agriculture	−2.0	9.6	−1.3	−1.4	−5.7	−7.0
Non-agrarian	−0.7	5.0	6.1	4.6	5.8	4.1
Manufacturing	−3.4	1.7	4.3	2.1	3.4	2.8
Construction	−4.8	7.4	11.9	10.3	11.1	7.6
Services	1.4	6.3	6.1	4.8	6.0	4.0
Total	−0.9	2.4	4.9	3.7	4.1	2.6

[1] For 1985-86: 1980 market prices; for 1987-90: 1986 market prices.
Source: *Labour Force Survey* and *National Accounts*.

jobs after 1981, as public sector employment rose. The share of professional and technical workers in total employment rose by 3 percentage points (from less than 6 per cent to almost 9 per cent).

The recovery of employment (1985-90)

Starting in mid-1985, the declining trend of employment began to reverse itself (see figure 1) paving the way for unprecedented growth in aggregate employment. The general economic recovery was a very important factor in this new trend, for GDP started growing at rates unknown in the previous ten years (see table 7). A relevant point in this connection is the relatively slow growth of measured productivity, which implies that the observed "employment-output elasticity" was much higher than could have been expected from the previous years of economic crisis.

At first, the employment recovery was seen by observers as something exceptional, whose explanation was not altogether clear and whose persistence was seen as very unlikely. In 1990, five years after it had begun, the recovery was seen as part of a new expansionary wave of the Spanish economy, which was expected to last several more years. In fact, economic activity stagnated in 1991 and 1992 to the point that employment decreased by 170,000 in the 15 months to March 1992 and unemployment has started rising again to a rate of 17.5 per cent at the end of the first quarter of 1992.

Figure 4 shows the evolution of employment by broad economic sectors between 1977 and 1990, using 1977 as the base year for comparison. Agricultural

Figure 4.   Evolution of employment by broad economic sectors, Spain, 1977-90

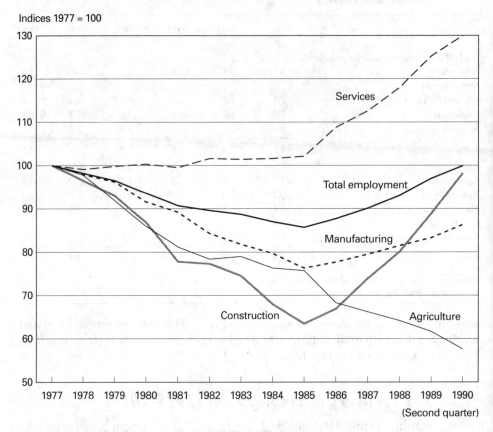

Indices 1977 = 100

employment decreased in the five years to 1990, at an average rate of about 4 per cent per year, reducing its share to 12 per cent of total employment. This share is still higher than elsewhere in Europe, which implies that further declines should be expected in the future. Construction, the sector which experienced the sharpest employment drop in the 1975-85 period, showed the most impressive employment growth in 1985-90. In 1986, employment in construction increased by 7.4 per cent; in 1987, 11.9 per cent; in 1988, 10.3 per cent; in 1989, 11.1 per cent; and in 1990, 7.6 per cent. In manufacturing, the recovery was milder, with employment increasing at an average annual rate of about 2.5 per cent in 1985-90. Finally, employment in services, which rose modestly during the employment crisis period, increased sharply at an average annual rate of about 6 per cent. Overall, this sector represents about two-thirds of the recovery in employment of 1985-89, the increase being most marked in the private sector, trade and tourism and "other services" (mostly personal services).

There are several noteworthy features of the change in employment distribution by occupation during the period of employment recovery (table 6). The category "Production (non-agricultural) workers" (blue-collar workers) has greatly

Figure 5.   Average yearly percentage change in employment by work status, 1976-85 and 1987-90

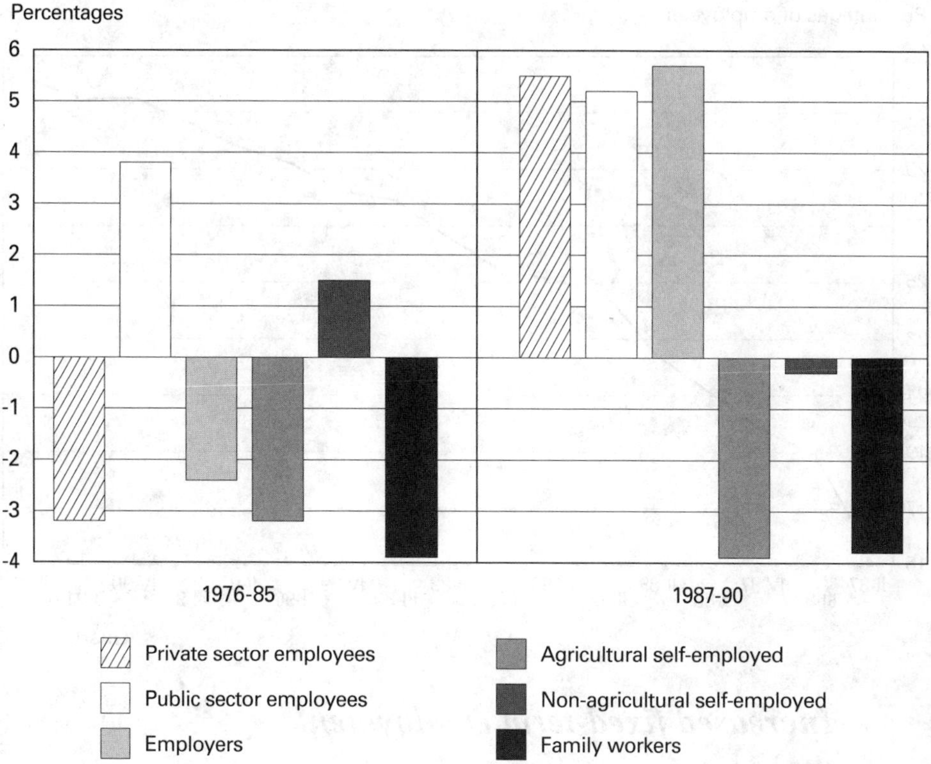

Percentages

Private sector employees

Public sector employees

Employers

Agricultural self-employed

Non-agricultural self-employed

Family workers

expanded, accounting for almost half the total increase in non-agricultural employment, though without so far regaining its 1981 employment share. White-collar occupations also increased substantially, the only exception being unskilled service workers. The category of "professional and technical staff" was again the most dynamic, accounting for 25 per cent of the increase in non-agricultural employment and bringing its share of total employment to about 10 per cent.

Finally, regarding the distribution of employment by work status, figure 5 depicts the average annual growth rates of the six groups distinguished in table 5. While during the crisis period, self-employment and jobs in the public sector moderated the sharp rise in unemployment, private sector employment has been the most dynamic factor during the recovery. Public sector jobs have continued to rise steadily but non-agricultural self-employment has stagnated. As usually happens during economic booms, therefore, the employment share of self-employment decreased while the share of wage-earners increased. These shifts also suggest, however, that there has been no large scale "decentralization" of production.

Figure 6.   Percentage of employees with a fixed-term contract, Spain, 1987-91

Percentages of employees

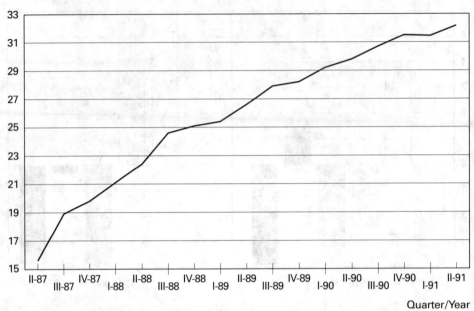

Quarter/Year

Increased fixed-term employment

One of the most striking changes in employment during the recovery has been the increase of temporary or fixed-term contracts. We shall deal with this issue at length in Chapter 4. Here we merely present the basic data.

Fixed-term employment contracts existed in Spain even during the Franco era. However, their use was somehow restricted until 1984, when the Spanish Government introduced new legal regulations on the matter (see Chapter 4). Since then, fixed-term employment has increased markedly to reach over 30 per cent of employment (see figure 6).

There are several interesting facts in the evolution of fixed-term employment. As in other countries, the main statistical source to analyse the evolution and composition of employment in Spain is the labour force survey. Unfortunately, the survey began to cover employment under fixed-term contracts only from the second quarter of 1987. Part (a) of table 8 shows the percentage of temporary employment in the main industrial sectors in the four years 1987-90. Since 1987, this percentage has doubled from about 15 per cent to over 30 per cent (see figure 6). Agriculture and fishing, followed by construction, are the activities with the highest proportion of workers employed under fixed-term contracts; these two sectors made most use of temporary contracts allowed by labour law before 1984. However, the increase in the share of fixed-term employment is also very large in manufacturing, in trade, communications and transport and in services.

Table 8. *Percentage of fixed-term workers according to the* **Labour Force Survey** *and the* **Bank** *of Spain survey, by main industrial sectors*

(a) *Labour Force Survey* data (second quarter)

	1987	1988	1990
Agriculture and fishing	39.67	47.39	50.57
Energy and water	4.10	7.30	9.31
Mining	1.14	4.95	5.73
Manufacturing durables	8.51	14.28	22.13
Manufacturing non-durables	15.99	24.72	29.75
Construction	29.48	42.31	54.13
Trade, communications and transport	17.13	23.94	31.50
Other services	11.17	16.50	22.55
Total	15.60	22.38	29.84

(b) Bank of Spain survey data

	1985	1987	1988	1990
Agriculture and fishing	7.61	8.76	10.06	10.78
Energy and water	2.68	3.01	3.24	3.23
Mining	2.71	2.99	4.64	6.07
Manufacturing durables	2.69	3.01	4.17	5.15
Manufacturing non-durables	6.15	6.95	8.92	10.65
Construction	34.69	38.44	38.56	41.55
Trade, communications and transport	6.58	10.14	12.98	14.57
Other services	8.45	8.64	10.40	11.01
Total	7.16	8.48	10.05	11.50

An additional statistical source to analyse the evolution of employment under fixed-term contracts is provided by the Bank of Spain's survey of company balance sheets. The labour force of the firms covered by this survey represents about 15 per cent of the total labour force (see Jimeno and Toharia, 1991b). These are mainly large firms between 1984 and 1988 where the percentage of workers under fixed-term employment contracts is lower, as presented in part (b) of table 8. Apart from the problems with the statistical sources, we draw two conclusions from the comparison. First, the increase in fixed-term employment began before the economic recovery of 1986. Second, since the proportion of temporary workers increased much more mildly in the large firms existing in 1984 sampled by the Bank of Spain, the most significant increases must have occurred in small and new firms.

Table 9 breaks down permanent and fixed-term employment by gender and by full- and part-time work. As can be seen, the number of male full-time permanent employees actually decreased sharply between 1987 and 1988 and more gently thereafter. The number of female full-time permanent and temporary workers increased, the number of female permanent part-time workers decreased and there was a rise in the number of women employed under part-time fixed-term

Table 9.   Number of permanent and fixed-term, full-time and part-time employees, Spain, 1987-90 (second quarter, thousands)

	Permanent		Fixed term		Total
	Full-time	Part-time	Full-time	Part-time	
Men					
1987	4 754.7	38.3	758.4	51.0	5 602.4
1988	4 578.4	32.3	1 144.0	45.2	5 799.9
1989	4 561.4	27.5	1 453.6	34.2	6 076.7
1990	4 520.6	22.7	1 706.7	42.0	6 292.0
Women					
1987	1 669.5	173.2	300.3	116.2	2 259.2
1988	1 641.9	168.4	519.8	142.4	2 472.5
1989	1 722.2	141.6	688.5	158.4	2 710.7
1990	1 775.4	148.1	820.4	181.3	2 925.2
Both sexes					
1987	6 424.1	211.6	1 058.7	167.2	7 861.6
1988	6 220.4	200.6	1 663.8	187.6	8 272.4
1989	6 283.5	169.2	2 142.1	192.6	8 787.4
1990	6 296.0	170.8	2 527.1	223.3	9 217.2

Source: *Labour Force Survey.*

employment contracts. However, table 9 shows the small and decreasing importance of part-time work, even for workers employed under fixed-term contracts.

The persistence of unemployment

The third main characteristic of the Spanish experience has been the only modest reduction in unemployment, despite the employment surge which began in 1985. This persistence of unemployment raises two issues. First, one needs to address the reasons which have prevented the increase of employment of almost 2 million jobs between 1985 and 1990 being translated into a commensurate reduction in unemployment (joblessness fell by only 600,000). Table 10 presents a basic summary of the figures on labour force, employment and unemployment during the recovery, comparing them with those observed during the crisis. Thus, while the labour force increased mildly during the crisis, it took off in 1985-90, particularly for women. Despite the fact that employment growth was equally shared between men and women, male unemployment decreased substantially but female unemployment increased. We shall return to this development and in general to the incidence of unemployment in Chapter 2.

Second, the macroeconomic aspects of this persistence — that is, the relationship between unemployment, wages and inflation — need to be analysed. It is often argued that the equilibrium unemployment rate has increased and, hence,

Table 10. Labour force, employment and unemployment by gender, Spain, 1977-91

	Absolute numbers			Average yearly variation			
	Thousands			Thousands		Percentages	
	1977	1985	1991	1977-85	1985-91	1977-85	1985-91
Males							
Labour force	9 323.7	9 410.3	9 708.0	10.8	49.6	0.12	0.52
Employment	8 908.5	7 629.1	8 549.2	−159.9	153.4	−1.92	1.92
Unemployment	415.2	1 781.2	1 158.8	170.7	−103.7	19.97	−6.91
Unemployment rate (%)	4.5	18.9	11.9				
Females							
Labour force	3 875.9	4 303.1	5 302.4	53.4	166.6	1.32	3.54
Employment	3 666.3	3 150.3	4 073.0	−64.5	153.8	−1.88	4.37
Unemployment	209.6	1 152.8	1 229.4	117.9	12.8	23.75	1.08
Unemployment rate (%)	5.4	26.8	23.2				
Both sexes							
Labour force	13 199.6	13 713.4	15 010.4	64.2	216.2	0.48	1.52
Employment	12 574.8	10 779.4	12 622.2	−224.4	307.1	−1.91	2.67
Unemployment	624.8	2 934.0	2 388.2	288.6	−91.0	21.33	−3.37
Unemployment rate (%)	4.7	21.4	15.9				

Source: *Labour Force Survey.*

the increases in actual unemployment just followed that equilibrium rate and persisted. This is a recurring topic in the discussion about the persistence of European unemployment in general. We shall deal with this notion in Chapter 3.

Unemployment and labour market flexibility: Explaining the Spanish experience

One conclusion from the foregoing analysis is that the evolution of unemployment in Spain differs from that of other Western European countries, mainly in the employment shifts described (destruction of jobs from 1975 to 1985 followed by an impressive recovery from 1985 to 1990). In fact, as the analysis of labour force participation in Chapter 2 will show, labour supply forces actually checked the increase in unemployment during the crisis of the late 1970s and early 1980s.

Thus, after a review of the Spanish experience of the 20 years to 1990, any account of the evolution of Spanish unemployment must provide explanations for the following:

  (i)   the big employment losses of the 1975-85 period;
 (ii)   the strong employment recovery during the second half of the 1980s;
(iii)   the persistence of unemployment despite this strong employment recovery.

One of the most influential explanations of the 1975-85 employment crisis is that the Spanish labour market was very inflexible. There are two strands to this argument. On the one hand, wages did not respond to the fall in national income suffered by the Spanish economy because of the oil shocks. On the other hand, firms could not adjust their workforces quickly and easily (i.e. cheaply), so that they were forced into loss and bankruptcy. As for the employment recovery, it is argued that wages finally fell (particularly in 1984) and that employment arrangements were made much more flexible when the Government introduced the 1984 labour law reforms to ease the use of fixed-term contracts. Finally, it is maintained that, even after these reforms, the Spanish labour market lacks sufficient flexibility, which explains why Spain still has a very high unemployment rate (around 17.5 per cent of the labour force at the end of the first quarter of 1992).

In this book we shall argue, on the contrary, that wages cannot be totally blamed for the employment losses of the 1975-85 period, though they have behaved moderately throughout the 1980s (see Chapter 3). In addition, we shall argue that employment rigidity was not as important during the crisis as has been suggested (see Chapter 4) and that while the introduction of fixed-term contracts may have helped employment recovery, it cannot be given full credit for that. Finally, on the influence of wage and employment rigidities on unemployment, we take a sceptical view: while it may be true that these rigidities still exist, and we shall point to some of them regarding both wages and employment, the Spanish economy could not have created more employment over the recovery years than it did, even if those rigidities had been removed. To maintain, as some do, that Spanish unemployment is high because wages are not sufficiently responsive is simply to miss the point and, in any case, one needs to explain what are the reasons for wages not to adjust.

We conclude this chapter by providing a brief account of the factors which we believe help explain the Spanish experience, beyond lack of flexibility.

(i)   The employment crisis was the consequence of the coincidence of domestic political and economic reform (after the breakdown of the Francoist social and economic models) and of the international economic crisis (caused by the two oil shocks of the mid-1970s and early 1980s).

The Francoist model of economic development began to break down at the beginning of the 1970s. Even before General Franco's death, social pressure had already brought about some of the changes that would later, with the advent of democracy, become more widespread and more solidly entrenched. These gains, achieved in the "protodemocratization" phase, could not be suppressed by the Franco regime because their causes were linked to causes of the boom years of the 1960s (such as tourism) and the expansion of the European economy. Thus, further overt and repressive actions on the Government's part would have endangered the economic boom.

On the other hand, the adverse supply shocks that precipitated the international economic crisis hit the Spanish economy harder than other European countries. Spain was, and still is, strongly dependent on imported oil products so that the increase in the oil price had adverse effects on most Spanish firms. Additionally, increases in real wages, a trend that had begun in 1970, were inevitable in a period of political turmoil when unions began to organize. Finally, economic policy was ineffective. Only in 1977 were contractionary measures implemented.

One consequence of the economic crisis was the decrease in demand. Domestic demand showed signs of saturation at the beginning of the 1970s and the most developed sectors were worst hit by this fall in demand. Furthermore, the economy could not continue to grow with a production structure that was so strongly protected from outside competition. The most modern and dynamic businesses could only prosper by branching out into bigger markets. This outward expansion was incompatible with a protectionist policy. Outward expansion (or at least the recognition that it was inevitable) thus heralded the downfall of businesses based on the existence of cheap labour and the non-existence of outside competition, which would not or could not adapt to the new situation.

Thus the foremost cause of employment losses in the 1975-85 period was the inefficiency and weakness of most Spanish firms, whose viability was based on the existence of cheap labour and lack of competition, and the change in the economic and political environment. The coincidence of the final breakdown of the Franco regime and the international economic crisis accentuated the impact. Additionally, uncertainty as to the system of economic relations which would prevail after the dictatorship lasted well beyond 1980 and, in any case, was not resolved at the time of the second oil shock.

(ii) The employment recovery from 1986 to 1990 had its origin in a demand boom to which exports and investment in infrastructure contributed significantly. A number of other factors can be tentatively adduced.

First, the Spanish recovery was part of the general economic expansion of the western world, which began in 1983 and affected Spain with some delay. Export demand was an important locomotive element across these countries. Secondly, the reduction of energy prices in 1985 also played a key part in an economy very dependent on energy imports, as Spain was and is. Spain's accession to the EC also was a dynamizing factor, opening up markets and fostering economic activity in general.

Second, there has been a general recovery of business profits, in large part the result of the wage restraint achieved through the social pacts reached each year (with the exceptions of 1984 and since 1987) between workers' and employers' organizations, and also on several occasions with the Government. This has led to increased investment demand, which grew in real terms from 1985 to 1990 after years of decline. Throughout the 1980s, unit labour costs have shown negative or very small positive growth rates (we shall return to this point in Chapter 3).

Finally, two kinds of government policies seem to have played important roles. First, in 1985, a government decree deregulated the market for rented dwellings and introduced tax exemptions for housing investment, while increasing taxes on financial assets. The combined result of these measures (together, probably, with Spain's accession to the EC) led to a skyrocketing of house prices and spurred construction activity, which, as we saw above, was a big contributor to recovery of both output and employment. Public investment in infrastructure (promoted and partly financed by the EC) has also been important. Second, in late 1984, parliament passed a major reform of the Workers' Statute *(Ley del Estatuto de los Trabajadores)*. This was designed to encourage new contractual forms of employment, such as fixed-term and part-time contracts which, although in existence since 1977, and indeed earlier under Franco, were either restricted or not clearly regulated. As already mentioned, the effects of this "flexibilization" of employment arrangements are controversial and will be dealt with in Chapter 4.

(iii) The high and persistent unemployment problem has two origins. Some weaknesses of the Spanish productive structure, which still remain, are behind the lack of an adequate number of jobs. On the other hand, some labour market institutions prevent the labour market from working as efficiently as it should. In particular, the behaviour of labour supply is particularly affected by some of these institutions and is often cited as the main reason for equilibrium unemployment being so high, which translates into high and persistent unemployment. We shall discuss these issues in Chapter 3.

(iv) Finally, there is the role played by employment policies in response to these developments, which we shall tackle in Chapter 5. In general, this policy can be labelled as *"passive and ineffective"*. While employment subsidies were available for production sectors in special difficulties, the main intervention to boost employment has been the promotion of fixed-term contracts. On the other hand, the unemployment protection system, the education system and vocational training programmes present widespread drawbacks, which do not ease the transition to a low unemployment situation.

Notes

[1] Some of this description draws on Fina (1987). We are grateful to him for allowing us to do so.

[2] Statistical Appendix to *Papeles de Economía Española*, No. 12-13, pp. 93-106; Ministerio de Trabajo y Seguridad Social, 1985; and *Boletín de Estadísticas Laborales*.

[3] Between 1970 and March 1981 the population in "rural zones" (towns with less than 2,000 inhabitants) roughly doubled from 3,744,500 or 11 per cent of total population to 7,588,800 or 20.1 per cent of total population.

[4] This figure comes from the standardized series of the Ministry of the Economy (see table 5). The OECD figure for 1979-87 is 3.2 per cent (see table 4).

Chapter 2

The incidence of unemployment

This paper is fascinating, elegant and quite informative. However, I am not sure that we yet know (or ever will) why Spanish unemployment is so extraordinarily high. (R. Layard's comments on Bentolila and Blanchard, 1990, published in the same issue of *Economic Policy*, April, p. 271.)

Introduction

In Chapter 1, we saw the tremendous shifts of employment which Spain experienced in the 20 years to 1990. While the fall in employment caused an almost one-for-one increase in unemployment during the 1975-85 period, the post-1985 recovery reduced it only moderately. The purpose of this chapter is to discuss the incidence of unemployment, first analysing labour force participation and later turning to a number of specific dimensions of participation and unemployment rates, including:

– sex and age differentials;
– regional disparities;
– first-job seekers;
– the duration of unemployment.

We conclude with some extrapolations as to future job creation needs if unemployment is to be reduced, given the demographic trends and some plausible estimates as to the behaviour of participation rates.

General overview

In Chapter 1, we divided the past 20 years into three sub-periods to look at the evolution of the labour force, employment and unemployment (figure 1). Four ratios can be used to summarize this process:

– the overall participation rate (L/P);
– the standard unemployment rate (U/L);
– the employment-population ratio (E/P);
– the unemployment-population ratio, which might be termed the "absolute unemployment rate" (U/P).

These indicators are related to each other. For example, the absolute unemployment rate is equal to the difference between the participation rate and the

Figure 7.   Labour force participation rate and employment-population ratio, Spain, 1970-90

Percentages

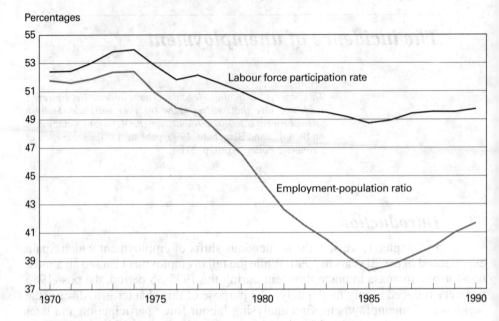

employment-population ratio. It is also equal to the participation rate times the standard unemployment rate. Two implications follow from this analysis:

(1)   if the participation rate remains constant, changes in the absolute and the standard unemployment rate will mirror that of the employment-population ratio;

(2)   if the participation rate remains constant, the standard and the absolute unemployment rates will tend to vary together.

These considerations are highly relevant to the Spanish case, as labour force participation has played a key role in the evolution of unemployment. Figure 7 shows changes in the overall participation rate and the employment-population ratio between 1970 and 1990 (as mentioned above, the difference between the two is the absolute unemployment rate). The main conclusion that can be drawn from the chart is that the overall participation rate (defined here in terms of the population aged 16 years and over) has tended to follow the economic cycle. During the crisis, it fell from a high of 54 per cent in 1974 to a low of 49 per cent in 1985. During the recovery, the global participation rate increased rapidly at first, slowing in the last two years. It now stands at just 50 per cent. Since Spain has one of the lowest participation rates of all western countries, this development is all the more surprising. Later in this chapter, we shall show that differences by age and gender have played a key role. On the other hand, the employment-population ratio declined continuously during the 1970s and first half of the 1980s, the period of employment crisis, and increased subsequently, thus mirroring the evolution of employment.

Figure 8.   *Unemployment rates in Spain, 1970-90: Standard, absolute and potentially observed if labour force participation rate had remained at its 1974 level*

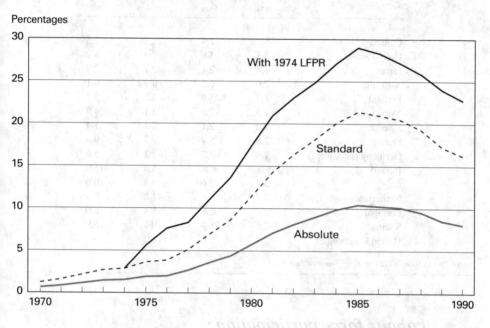

Turning now to unemployment, figure 8 shows what happened to both the standard and the absolute rates in the 20 years to 1990. In order to bring out fully the influence of labour force behaviour, it also shows what would have happened if the participation rate had remained constant at its 1974 level. On this basis, unemployment would have reached 28 per cent in 1985, and 23 per cent in 1990. These figures should be taken as illustrative rather than as a measure of "potential unemployment"; not all the observed change in labour force participation can be considered a response to the economic crisis, since some of it would have taken place in any case. The size of the fall in participation since 1974, however, makes our analysis at least a crude approximation.

Table 11 gives standardized unemployment rates in a selected number of OECD countries over the period 1974-79. The countries in the table have been divided into three groups, non-European, Scandinavian, and other European countries. Spain has the dubious honour of being the country with the highest unemployment rate, though the gap between it and Ireland has diminished since 1984.

Table 11. Standardized unemployment rates in selected OECD countries, 1974-89

	1974	1979	1984	1989
Canada	5.3	7.4	11.2	7.5
United States	5.5	5.8	7.4	5.2
Japan	1.4	2.1	2.7	2.3
Australia	2.6	6.2	8.9	6.1
Finland	1.7	5.9	5.2	3.4
Norway	1.5	2.0	3.1	4.9
Sweden	2.0	2.1	3.1	1.4
France	2.8	5.9	9.7	9.4
Germany (Fed. Rep.)	1.6	3.2	7.1	5.6
Ireland	n.a.	n.a.	15.4	15.0
Italy	5.3	7.6	9.4	10.9
Netherlands	2.7	5.4	11.8	9.3
Portugal	n.a.	n.a.	8.4	5.0
Spain	2.6	8.4	19.7	16.9
United Kingdom	2.9	5.0	11.7	6.9

Source: OECD, *Quarterly Labour Force Statistics*. Paris, 1990.

Labour force participation: Age and sex differentials

Trends in participation rates and unemployment are closely related to the labour force behaviour of different demographic groups. In this section, we analyse age and gender data in 1964, 1974, 1984 and 1989.

Table 12 presents trends in male and female participation rates (in relation to population aged 15 and over and to the working-age population aged 15-64). While male participation rates have tended to decrease steadily, female rates have followed a pro-cyclical pattern: they increased during the growth periods of the 1960s and early 1970s, decreased during the crisis and have risen sharply in the recent recovery. The picture does not change much for participation rates in relation to the working-age population, although for males the decline after 1979 was modest and there was a slight recovery in the second half of the 1980s. However, these trends conceal important age differences which imply significant and long-lasting changes in labour market behaviour, particularly of women.

Before turning to an analysis by age, it is worth putting the overall figures in an international perspective. Table 13 presents a comparison with the same OECD countries shown in table 11. While men's participation has followed the more or less general declining trend observed in other countries, and its level is not out of line with those elsewhere, female participation is very low, second only to Ireland due to the sharp rise in Spain in recent years.

Table 12. Male and female participation rates with respect to population aged 15 years and over and aged 15-64, Spain, 1964-89

Year	Males		Females	
	15 and over	15-64	15 and over	15-64
1964	84.0	91.3	22.9	25.6
1969	82.0	90.0	23.2	26.5
1974	78.4	87.2	29.0	33.8
1979	71.8	81.4	27.2	32.6
1984	69.3	79.9	27.7	34.1
1989	67.9	80.0	32.9	41.1

Note: Participation rates refer to 16 years and over and 16-64 years respectively in 1984 and 1989.
Source: *Labour Force Survey*, original data.

Table 13. Participation rates by gender in 15 selected OECD countries, 1974-89

	Males				Females			
	1974	1979	1984	1989	1974	1979	1984	1989
Canada	87.8	87.6	85.9	87.0	46.1	56.1	62.1	68.2
United States	89.1	88.3	87.0	87.8	53.9	60.5	64.3	69.4
Japan	90.1	89.3	88.4	87.2	52.4	54.7	57.2	59.3
Australia	90.3	87.3	85.4	85.4	48.7	50.2	52.6	60.6
Finland	85.1	82.3	81.9	81.0	67.5	68.9	73.1	73.5
Norway	86.7	86.7	90.7	87.6	51.2	62.2	68.2	72.9
Sweden	90.5	89.9	87.2	88.7	66.3	74.4	78.8	83.2
France	85.7	83.3	78.6	76.8	51.9	55.4	56.1	57.6
Germany (Fed. Rep.)	88.0	84.5	79.9	n.a.	49.8	49.6	49.8	n.a.
Ireland[1]	91.1	89.0	86.6	83.9	34.8	35.2	36.9	37.5
Italy	79.7	81.1	78.0	76.9	29.5	38.2	40.3	44.0
Netherlands	83.0	78.5	76.5	79.7	31.5	34.5	40.7	51.1
Portugal	95.3	91.2	87.0	84.3	52.1	55.4	59.4	58.7
Spain	90.9	88.8	84.0	81.1	34.9	34.3	34.7	41.3
United Kingdom	93.1	91.9	87.7	86.3	58.0	61.2	61.9	66.0

[1] Data for Ireland correspond to 1975 and 1988 instead of 1974 and 1989.
Source: OECD: *Labour Force Statistics, 1966-88*, Paris, 1990.

Figure 9 presents age-specific male participation rates in 1964, 1974, 1984 and 1989.[1] It shows that the reduction of the overall rate has been due to steadily falling participation rates of youngsters and older workers. For youngsters, lower labour market participation is connected to expansion of the educational system, and it is noteworthy that the participation rate of teenagers continued to fall during the recent recovery. For young adults (20-24 years), participation rates were unchanged between 1984 and 1989.

Figure 9.   Male age-specific labour force participation rates, 1964-89

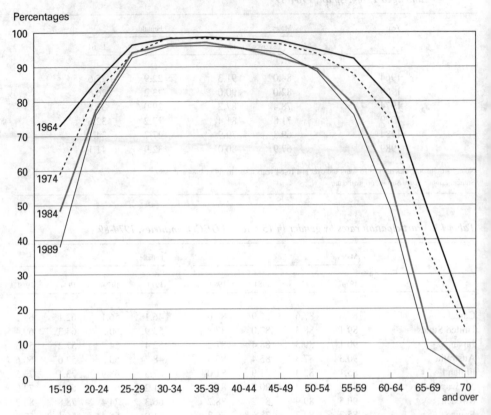

Percentages

At the other end of the age spectrum, the general trend towards earlier retirement was clearly accentuated during the economic crisis of the late 1970s and early 1980s, when the participation rates of those over 45 dropped sharply. The welfare policies adopted by successive governments undoubtedly eased this process. In the post-1984 recovery, participation rates of older males continued to decline, but more slowly and only noticeably for those over 55.

The evolution of female participation rates (figure 10) shows a rather interesting pattern. Between 1964 and 1974, the entire participation profile shifted upward. The crisis brought about important changes, as young women already in the labour market stayed longer than before, so inflating the profile in the central age groups (25-40 years). On the other hand, the teenage participation rate fell as steeply as for boys, and rates for older women also declined. The recovery was accompanied by sharply increasing female participation rates, especially in the central age groups, but with a different profile: in 1989, for the first time, the highest participation rate moved to the right, to the 25-29 age group from the 20-24 group.

The situation of both youngsters and older workers is thus crucial if one is to understand the behaviour of overall participation rates. It is worth completing our analysis by studying the labour force status of these groups: employed,

Figure 10.   Female age-specific labour force participation rates, 1964-89

Percentages

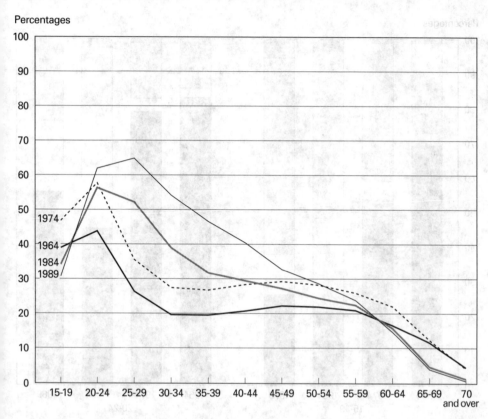

unemployed, students and others out of the labour force. Figure 11 presents this information for civilian males aged 15(16)-19 and 20-24 years for the same four years.[2] Figure 12 presents similar data for females. The former figure shows the increasing proportion of students and the decreasing proportion of the employed among male teenagers. The big jump in unemployment between 1974 and 1984 later gives way to an increase in the proportion of both the employed and students. Similar though less marked trends are observed for the 20-24 age group. For females (figure 12), the most striking feature is the drop in the "other non-labour force" category, mostly housewives or housekeepers. The proportion has fallen from about half of young women in 1964 to 10-20 per cent in 1989. The evolution of other categories is similar to that for men: a big increase in the proportion of students, and rising and falling unemployment during the crisis and recovery periods. However, there was an increase in the employment ratio of adult women during the first period of economic growth (1964-74), which was not the case for men.

Figure 13 presents a chart similar to figures 11 and 12 for older people aged 50-64. While in 1964 and 1974 over 90 per cent of men in this age group were employed, in 1984 the percentage had decreased by about 15 points and it did not rise in subsequent years despite the creation of many new jobs. Unemployment,

Figure 11.   Distribution of life situations of young males, 15(16)-19 and 20-24, Spain, 1964-89

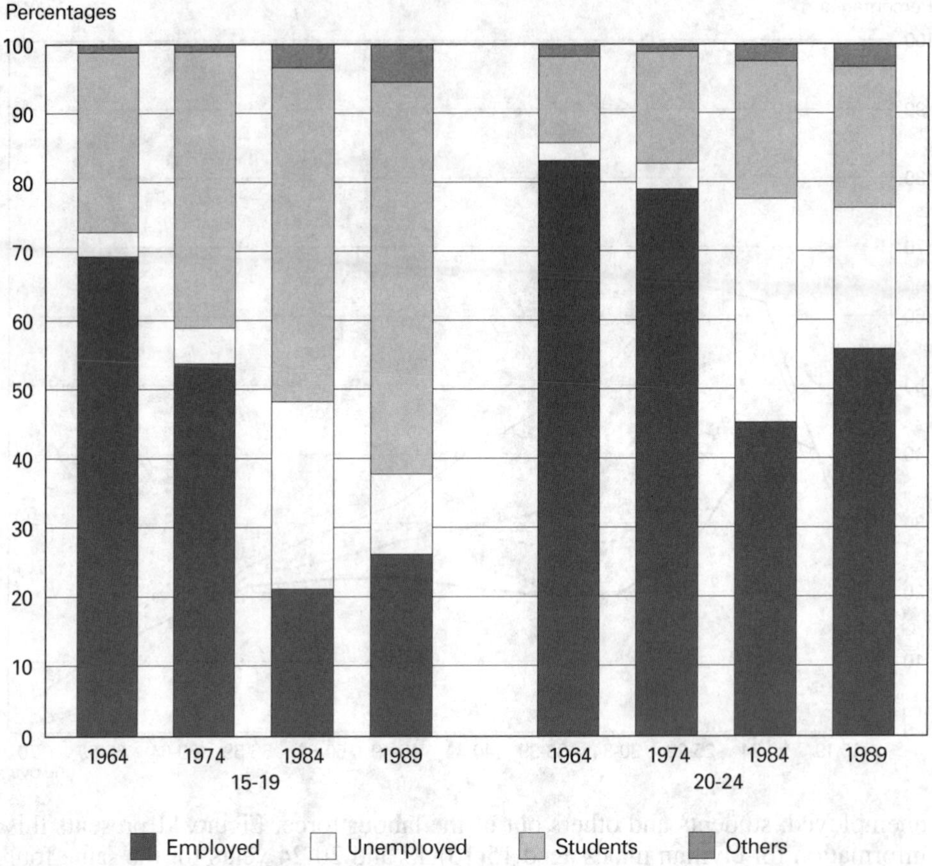

Percentages

on the other hand, reached a high level in 1984 and then fell back sharply. Thus, the phenomenon of ever earlier retirement has maintained its vigorous trend during the recent recovery. For women, the variations during the period 1964-89 are very limited, mostly due to their small proportion in the labour force.

The overall evolution of participation rates can, for the most part, be traced to the decreasing rates at both ends of the age distribution, offset by an increase in female rates in the central age groups. For youngsters, the extension of education has been the main factor behind the decrease in participation rates. While it might be argued that the increase in education rates during the crisis was related to unemployment, with discouraged unemployed or potentially unemployed youngsters deciding to further their education, the trend over the five years to 1989 confirms that education is a positive and attractive option rather than a negative one.

Figure 12.   Distribution of life situations of young females, 15(16)-19 and 20-24, Spain, 1964-89

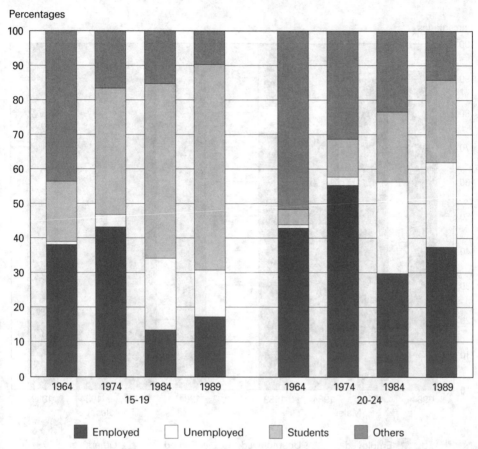

Percentages

Employed   Unemployed   Students   Others

For older workers, early retirement is behind the trend in participation rates. Here, the argument that retirement acts as a disguise for unemployment may be true. Many opting for retirement might have remained in the labour market had they expected to stay employed. Instead, they found themselves redundant, perhaps after a long career, and with little prospect of finding a new job.

The result of this process has been that the evolution of the Spanish labour force has been much more pro-cyclical than in other Western countries. As the figures in table 14 show, the labour force in Spain grew more slowly than in other Western European countries during the 1975-85 period. Conversely, it has grown faster in the recent recovery period.

Figure 13.   Distribution of life situations of older people aged 50-64, by gender, Spain, 1964-89

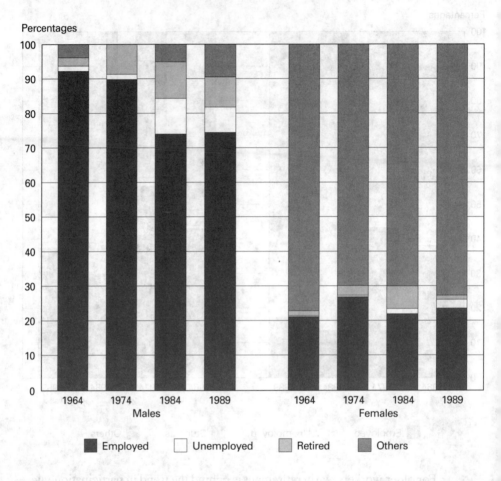

Percentages

Males   Females

■ Employed   □ Unemployed   ▨ Retired   ▨ Others

Table 14.   Growth of the labour force in various OECD regions and countries, various periods, 1960-88 (average annual percentage)

	1960-68	1968-73	1973-79	1979-88
OECD	0.9	1.3	1.3	1.3
EC	0.2	0.5	0.6	0.9
Spain	0.7	0.9	0.1	1.2
Germany (Fed. Rep.)	−0.1	0.7	−0.2	–
France	0.6	1.1	0.9	0.4
United Kingdom	0.4	0.2	0.6	0.6
Italy	−0.6	−0.2	1.1	1.0

Source: OECD, *Historical Statistics*, Paris, 1990.

Figure 14.   *Standard male unemployment rates by age, 1964-89*

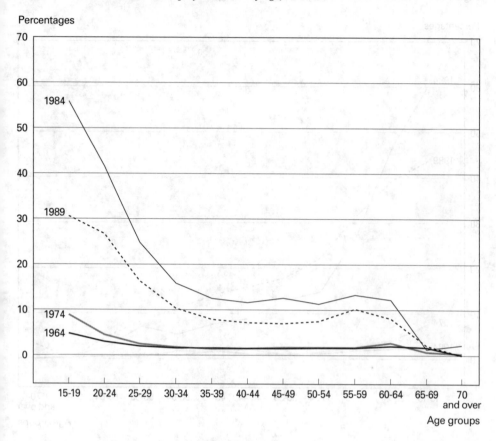

Percentages

Unemployment: Characteristics of the unemployed

The preceding section looked at the behaviour of labour force participation rates, which is essential to understand the changing incidence of unemployment in Spain. We now turn to a more direct analysis of the composition and characteristics of the unemployed. We first present the general evolution since 1964 of unemployment rates by age and gender, followed by a more detailed study of changes in the second half of the 1980s, when rapid growth of employment led to only moderate reductions in unemployment.

Figures 14 and 15 present unemployment rates by age and gender in 1964, 1974, 1984 and 1989. The former figure shows the tremendous rise in male unemployment rates between 1974 and 1984 for all age groups, but especially for youngsters, where it reached almost 60 per cent in spite of the substantial reduction in their participation rate. Between 1984 and 1989, male unemployment rates fell across the board, but the rates for teenagers and young adults fell fastest. For

Figure 15.   Standard female unemployment rates by age, 1964-89

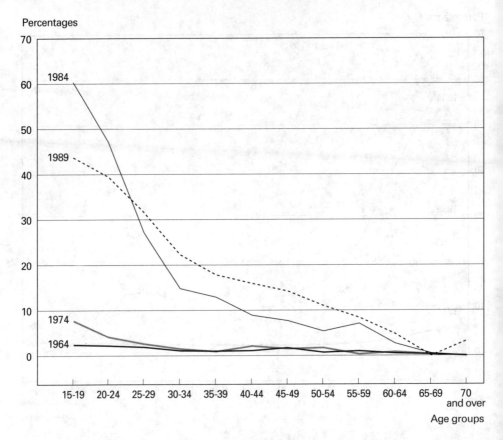

Percentages

women, the pattern is different (figure 15): while the youth unemployment rate (under 25) declined in the recovery, the adult rates increased quite substantially.

Turning to analysis of recent unemployment experience, we focus on the period 1987-90 (second quarter) for which homogeneous data exist.[3] The first question that ought to be addressed is: who are the unemployed? To answer such a question, table 15 presents a number of characteristics of the unemployed in 1987 and 1990. The analysis is carried out separately for four groups: males with and without past job experience, and females with and without past job experience. In addition to a number of basic characteristics related to age and education level, we have also included a number of other indicators relating to the family situation (not only the family position but also some characteristics of the household head where different from the unemployed person, as well as the existence of other unemployed in the family or the absence of an employed family member),[4] the willingness to accept a job under various circumstances and, in the case of those with past job experience, the reasons for leaving their job and the seniority in that job.[5]

Table 15(a).   Age characteristics of different groups of unemployed, Spain, 1987 and 1990

	Numbers (thousands)	%	Average age (years)	% under 22 years	% under 31 years	% over 47 years
1987						
Without work experience						
Men	457.2	100	21.0	60.2	97.9	0.0
Women	646.6	100	22.5	54.9	92.5	1.1
With work experience						
Men	1 169.5	100	36.0	12.6	45.2	25.4
Women	663.1	100	31.2	19.2	57.7	10.6
1990						
Without work experience						
Men	230.9	100	21.7	54.4	97.4	0.0
Women	460.7	100	24.7	39.7	84.5	2.1
With work experience						
Men	933.4	100	35.5	13.8	45.7	23.2
Women	813.1	100	31.5	15.8	55.2	10.0

Source: *Labour Force Survey.*

Three of the four groups under consideration shrank substantially between 1987 and 1990. Only the group of women with past job experience showed an increase, of 23 per cent; the number of their male counterparts declined by 20 per cent. Among those without past job experience both males and females showed big decreases, of 50 per cent for males and 30 per cent for females. As a result unemployment has become increasingly a feminine issue; in 1991 women represented almost 52 per cent of the total unemployed, though they accounted for only about one-third of those employed.

Looking at the age indicators in table 15(a), the most interesting results document the mild ageing between 1987 and 1990 of those unemployed without past job experience. For males, there seems to have been an increase in the number of jobless people in their twenties: those aged between 22 and 30 years represented 37.7 per cent in 1987, a proportion which had risen to 43 per cent by 1990. This may be due either to a slower rate of entry of teenagers into the labour market or to a displacement of young adults by teenagers in the rate of entry into employment; probably both factors have been at play. Among females, where this process is more marked, the proportion of jobless aged over 30 without past work experience rose from 7.5 per cent in 1987 to 15.5 per cent three years later.

The reverse process seems to have taken place among unemployed men with past job experience. Again this may be due to the outflow of older workers from unemployment to either employment or retirement. Again, both forces have probably been responsible. At any rate, the figures suggest that unemployed men with past job experience are not completely trapped in their situation: the decrease in their average age suggests renewal of their stock. These conclusions apply to a lesser extent to women, whose average age increased slightly.

Table 15(b).   Educational characteristics of different groups of unemployed, Spain, 1987 and 1990

	Average education level (years)	% with no education	% with at least secondary education	% students
1987				
Without work experience				
Men	8.7	2.1	9.0	15.3
Women	9.2	2.1	14.4	17.8
With work experience				
Men	5.9	19.7	3.8	2.4
Women	7.1	12.1	7.4	5.1
1990				
Without work experience				
Men	9.3	1.9	12.7	21.9
Women	9.5	3.2	16.2	17.8
With work experience				
Men	6.3	17.4	4.1	2.8
Women	7.6	9.3	7.1	4.8

Source: *Labour Force Survey.*

Regarding the level of education (table 15(b)), three trends can be observed. First, those unemployed without past job experience are more educated than their counterparts with job experience, mainly because they are much younger. Second, and more interestingly, the average level of education of all groups increased between 1987 and 1990. This result may be only partially related to age; among females, at least, the age structure of unemployed with past job experience has shifted upwards slightly. Third, women's level of education is higher than men's, which indicates that women who participate in the labour market tend to be better educated than those who do not.

As for family position (table 15(c)), almost all the unemployed without past job experience live with their parents, especially males. However, an increasing proportion of females without job experience declared themselves as spouse of the household head. This may be due to the fact that being a housewife conflicts with job search rather than to an increase in the number of married women entering the labour market, as the absolute numbers of unemployed women who are spouses of the household head are virtually the same in 1987 and 1990. Those unemployed with past job experience are either household heads (in the case of males) or spouses (females) or children, the proportions remaining quite stable over time.

A very interesting result included in table 15(c) refers to the unemployment situation of the household head in the case of those unemployed who are either his/her spouse or children. Once again the incidence decreased quite substantially. Thus, while in 1987 the percentage of husbands of unemployed women who were also unemployed were 12 and 19 per cent (in the case of those without and with past job experience, respectively), the corresponding figures for 1990 were 11 and

Table 15(c).   Family characteristics of different groups of unemployed, Spain, 1987 and 1990

	% household heads (HH)	% spouse of HH	% spouses of HH with unemployed HH	% children of HH	% children of HH with unemployed HH	% in household with no employed	In house-hold with at least one other unemployed
1987							
Without work experience							
Men	2.0	0.1	–	93.9	11.6	24.8	47.1
Women	1.4	9.9	12.1	84.1	9.4	22.1	41.5
With work experience							
Men	50.4	0.8	–	41.5	11.9	49.4	37.4
Women	6.1	45.1	18.6	42.8	10.0	28.8	36.4
1990							
Without work experience							
Men	1.7	0.0	–	93.2	8.1	24.0	40.9
Women	2.4	16.5	10.9	77.1	7.9	20.1	36.4
With work experience							
Men	48.1	0.5	–	44.9	8.0	47.1	33.1
Women	6.7	46.4	14.9	42.6	6.5	25.0	26.9

Source: *Labour Force Survey.*

15 per cent. For children of the household head, the corresponding figures dropped from 10-12 per cent in 1987 to 6.5-8 per cent three years later.

We have also computed the general employment and unemployment situation of the unemployed's households. Thus, around half of unemployed males with past job experience had someone employed in their household (i.e. in half the cases there was no one employed in the household). This proportion was higher for unemployed women with job experience, and for both men and women first-job seekers, at between 75 and 80 per cent. These proportions rose slightly between 1987 and 1990.

The analysis can be completed with information on the existence of somebody else unemployed in the household. While 36-47 per cent of unemployed shared their situation with another family member in 1987, three years later the proportion had fallen to 27-41 per cent. The number of households hit by unemployment fell from 21.1 per cent in 1987 to 17.6 per cent three years later, while the proportion of households with someone unemployed but no one employed declined over the same period from 7.0 per cent to 5.3 per cent.[6]

Table 15(d) presents a number of indicators relating to the willingness of the unemployed to accept potential jobs. Of the four conditions set (change of residence, change of occupation, occupational downgrading and loss of earnings), the first appears to be the least acceptable, especially to women. But in all four cases, the unemployed seem to have become more restrictive on conditions. This may be interpreted as evidence that those who are less willing to accept changes in their working conditions are more likely to remain unemployed. But it might

Table 15(d). Job search characteristics of different groups of unemployed, Spain, 1987 and 1990

	% who would accept a job				% who would not accept a job			
	If it implied a change of residence	If it implied a change of occupation	With earnings lower than those corresponding to skill level	If it implied skill downgrading	If it implied a change of residence	If it implied a change of occupation	With earnings lower than those corresponding to skill level	If it implied skill downgrading
1987								
Without work experience								
Men	48.4	75.4	69.9	73.3	30.1	8.4	11.6	9.1
Women	29.9	71.0	66.0	69.6	48.1	11.6	13.5	11.6
With work experience								
Men	41.1	75.3	63.2	70.9	38.2	13.3	18.2	13.1
Women	23.5	74.6	58.4	64.9	59.9	12.7	19.8	15.6
1990								
Without work experience								
Men	38.5	68.4	55.4	60.6	29.1	6.9	14.3	11.4
Women	28.1	65.3	54.5	58.9	42.8	8.8	14.5	10.6
With work experience								
Men	37.9	71.7	52.4	60.2	36.4	9.8	20.0	14.7
Women	19.5	69.4	50.9	55.8	57.2	9.0	18.9	15.5

Source: Labour Force Survey.

Table 15(e).   *Work experience characteristics of different groups of unemployed, Spain, 1987 and 1990*

	Who left their jobs because of end of contract	Who left their jobs because of dismissals	% less than one year in previous job	% more than three years in previous job
1987				
Without work experience				
Men				
Women				
With work experience				
Men	56.1	29.4	56.1	22.9
Women	54.7	24.5	56.9	18.0
1990				
Without work experience				
Men				
Women				
With work experience				
Men	72.7	13.4	64.2	19.3
Women	71.2	10.9	64.0	12.5

Source: *Labour Force Survey.*

also be due to the fact that the economic upturn raised people's expectations (including those of the unemployed).

Finally, with respect to those unemployed with past job experience, table 15(e) provides information on the reason why they left their last job and the time spent in that job. The results suggest a clear increase in labour turnover related to the "atypical" contractual forms introduced in 1985. Thus, "end of contract" explains an increasing proportion of the flows from employment into unemployment, while dismissals (a form of job separation connected more with permanent jobs) have become less important. At the same time, the proportion of those flows corresponding to people who had been in their jobs for less than one year increases between 1987 and 1990 from 56 per cent to 64 per cent. It seems clear that the flow of people leaving employment to join the ranks of the unemployed is increasingly composed of people who had fixed-term contracts for less than a year.

Regional disparities

One interesting dimension for analysis of unemployment in Spain is whether or not all regions have been affected in a homogeneous way and the extent to which regional disparities widened or narrowed during different economic phases. Some Spanish authors (notably, Bentolila and Dolado, 1990) have noted the asymmetric behaviour of the dispersion of regional unemployment rates with respect to the trend of the national rate: while absolute dispersion has increased over the two decades to 1990, relative dispersion[7] decreased as national unemployment increased (up to 1985) and rose subsequently. Their analysis

Table 16. Unemployment rates and employment-population ratios by region, Spain, 1981-90

	1981	1985	1987	1990
Unemployment rates				
[Regions ranked according to their				
unemployment rate in 1990]				
* Andalucía	20.4	30.1	30.8	25.8
* Extremadura	16.7	27.8	25.7	25.3
* Canarias	17.0	26.8	25.2	23.0
País Vasco	16.3	23.9	23.0	19.3
* Asturias	11.9	18.6	19.5	17.3
Cantabria	10.2	15.6	18.4	16.7
* Murcia	13.0	20.3	21.1	15.7
* Castilla y León	10.6	18.3	17.4	15.5
* Com. Valenciana	13.6	21.3	19.8	14.0
* Castilla-La Mancha	14.3	17.0	15.0	13.2
Cataluña	15.4	22.8	21.5	12.6
Madrid	15.5	22.2	16.1	12.5
* Galicia	5.9	13.0	13.2	11.9
Navarra	13.1	19.0	15.0	10.9
Baleares	9.8	13.9	13.1	10.2
Aragón	12.0	17.8	12.5	9.3
Rioja (La)	7.6	17.4	13.1	7.3
SPAIN	14.4	21.9	20.6	16.3
Employment-population ratios				
[Regions ranked according to their				
employment-population ratio in 1990]				
* Andalucía	36.9	31.0	33.5	34.0
Aragón	34.6	30.6	32.0	34.9
* Asturias	37.7	36.0	37.4	38.7
Baleares	41.1	36.5	37.4	39.2
* Canarias	43.6	39.1	38.9	39.2
Cantabria	41.6	36.6	38.4	39.9
* Castilla-La Mancha	43.0	37.3	37.4	40.5
* Castilla y León	45.5	34.7	37.2	40.7
Cataluña	41.3	37.4	40.8	42.0
* Com. Valenciana	40.2	36.8	40.8	42.8
* Extremadura	40.6	37.1	38.9	42.9
* Galicia	44.4	37.7	40.5	43.1
Madrid	43.2	39.7	41.4	43.3
* Murcia	41.9	38.1	40.5	43.8
Navarra	50.4	47.6	45.9	45.5
País Vasco	43.3	38.0	40.9	46.3
Rioja (La)	43.6	41.6	43.0	46.9
SPAIN	41.2	37.8	38.7	41.3

Note: Asterisks indicate EC Objective-1 Region.
Source: *Labour Force Survey.*

indicates the problem of measuring dispersion when average figures vary considerably and the variables analysed are not smooth.[8]

At any rate, what seems clear is that unemployment rates show a wide variation between regions, a variation which has tended to persist, even though it is not clear whether it has increased or decreased. Table 16 presents unemployment rates in the 17 Spanish regions ("Autonomous Communities", as they are called in Spain, hereafter AC) in 1981, 1985, 1987 and 1990.[9] Given the pro-cyclical behaviour of participation rates, noted above, we have also included in the table the employment-population ratios. The regions appear ranked by their 1990 unemployment rate. Both indicators show persistent regional differentials. However, no clear pattern emerges; the regions with the highest unemployment rates do not tend to fare worse over time than those with a better unemployment performance. Moreover, the regions with the highest unemployment rates are not always those with the lowest per capita incomes: the European Community's Objective-1 regions (defined as those whose average per capita income is below 75 per cent of the EC average and indicated in the table by an asterisk) are not all at the top of the table of unemployment rankings. This raises interesting questions which are beyond the scope of this book. Nevertheless, the figures do suggest that the regional dimension is an important and rather poorly studied factor in understanding unemployment issues in Spain.

The problem of first-job seekers

As we have seen, unemployment rates among young people reached very high levels in Spain as a consequence of the deep crisis of the 1970s and 1980s. This undoubtedly created a problem of labour market integration for young people. What has happened in recent years? Have these "barriers to entry" been lowered?

Figure 16 shows the proportion of young (16-24 years) unemployed who have and have not had previous job experience. As the figure shows, the proportion of youngsters without past job experience fell dramatically during the period of employment recovery, even reaching a level below that prevailing in 1976, when the overall unemployment rate was very low. Thus, even though youth unemployment is still high in Spain, there are reasons to believe that problems of integration into the labour market eased substantially in the second half of the 1980s.

Long-term unemployment

A final aspect of the evolution and incidence of unemployment relates to long-term unemployment, which in Spain reaches substantial proportions. Table 17 presents two general views of this problem: on the one hand, the proportion of the long-term unemployed (LTU, those seeking a job for a year or more) and very long-term unemployed (VLTU, those seeking a job for two years or more) in the period 1987-91;[10] on the other, a longitudinal approach to calculate "survival probabilities" — the probability of remaining unemployed a year later — to throw light on the "duration dependence" of long-term unemployment.

Figure 16.   Proportion of unemployed aged 16-24 with and without past job experience, Spain, 1976-90

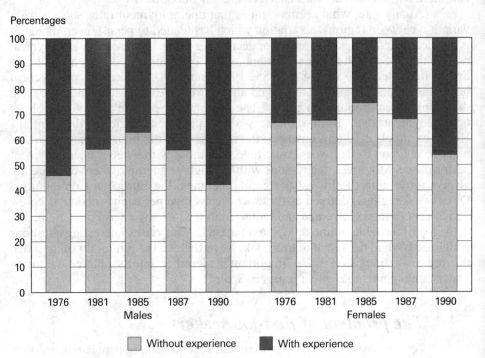

Percentages

As can be seen in table 17, the proportion of the LTU has fallen sharply, especially among men; this has also been true in the case of the VLTU for both men and women, despite the only modest reduction in overall unemployment rates. The view that long-term unemployment in Spain is a formidable problem which has even worsened in the last few years (a view, taken for example, in Andrés, García and Jiménez, 1990, and Layard, Nickell and Jackman, 1991) would not seem to be warranted by the data. Data on labour market flows into employment also lead to a similar conclusion (see Jimeno and Toharia, 1992).

On the other hand, we have also computed "survival probabilities" by comparing those looking for work for one to two years with those who reported 12 months earlier that they had been looking for work for less than a year (if all of them had remained unemployed, the two groups would have been the same). The calculations show that survival probabilities are lower for those with less "unemployment seniority", i.e. those unemployed for a shorter period seem to be able to escape from their situation more easily than those out of work for longer. The interesting fact, however, is that these survival probabilities tended to decline substantially between 1987 and 1991 for the two groups considered. It should also be pointed out that, among females, the differences between the probabilities for short-term and long-term unemployed are relatively small.

Table 17. Long-term unemployment: Percentage of total unemployment and transition probabilities, Spain, 1987-91 (second quarter)

Distribution of unemployed by duration (thousands)

	II-1987	II-1988	II-1989	II-1990	II-1991
Men					
0-11 months	631.1	646.0	581.5	604.1	649.0
12-23 months	274.4	240.6	217.5	192.4	205.2
2 years and over	703.5	595.7	453.0	345.3	288.6
Women					
0-11 months	367.5	430.2	417.1	486.1	480.6
12-23 months	245.2	258.5	236.5	245.3	253.0
2 years and over	690.0	697.5	622.1	531.3	479.1

Long-term unemployed (LTU) and very long-term
unemployed (VLTU) as % of total unemployment

	II-1987	II-1988	II-1989	II-1990	II-1991
Men					
LTU	60.8	56.4	53.6	47.1	43.2
VLTU	43.7	40.2	36.2	30.2	25.3
Women					
LTU	71.8	69.0	67.3	61.5	60.4
VLTU	53.0	50.3	48.8	42.1	39.5

Transition probabilities

	87-88	88-89	89-90	90-91
Men				
From 0-11 months to 12 months or more	38.1	33.7	33.1	34.0
From 12 months or more to 2 years or more	60.9	54.2	51.5	53.7
Women				
From 0-11 months to 12 months or more	70.3	55.0	58.8	52.0
From 12 months or more to 2 years or more	74.6	65.0	61.9	60.9

Source: Authors' calculations.

To get some historical perspective on these survival probabilities, figures 17 and 18 present trends since 1976 for both sexes. The methodological break of 1987 prevents linking the two portions of the figure. As can be seen, the survival probabilities tend to rise as the unemployment rate increases; however, with employment recovery, despite little reduction in the unemployment rate, the probabilities also tend to decrease, especially for males. For females, in general, developments have been worse, since survival probabilities have risen by more and showed a greater resistance to downward movement.

Figure 17.   "Survival probabilities" of unemployed males after 1 year (LTU) and 2 years (VLTU), Spain, 1977-90

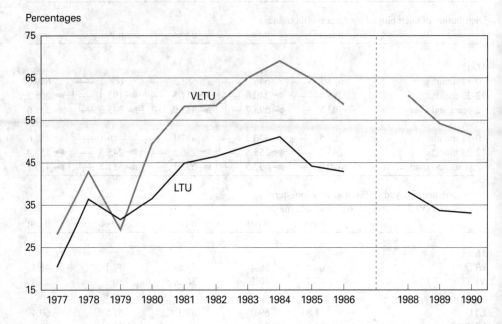

Figure 18.   "Survival probabilities" of unemployed females after 1 year (LTU) and 2 years (VLTU), Spain, 1977-90

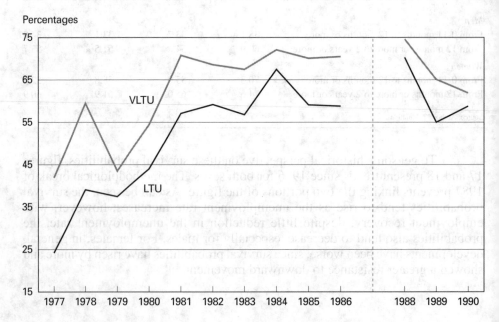

Figure 19.   Unemployment rates and proportion of long-term unemployment, by regions (Autonomous Communities), Spain, 1991 (second quarter)

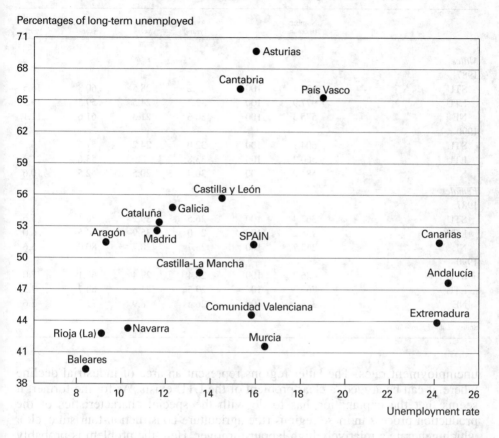

We have argued so far that the LTU have decreased in number quite substantially over the past few years. The question remains as to whether those remaining unemployed constitute a pool of "unemployable" people who cannot compete effectively in the labour market. To deal with this issue, we shall first consider the regional dimension and then turn to a comparison of the characteristics of the LTU versus other groups of workers.

In general terms, we would argue that long-term unemployment is not a very different problem from unemployment itself. If this is true, there should be a positive relationship between the unemployment rate and the percentage of the LTU at the regional level. Figure 19 presents data for the 17 Spanish regions in 1991 (second quarter). The data generally bear out the idea that unemployment and the LTU are positively correlated. There are, however, two groups of regions which are exceptions to this rule: the three southern regions (Andalucía, Extremadura and Canarias) where the proportion of the LTU is low compared to their very high unemployment rates, and three other regions (Asturias, Cantabria, País Vasco), all in the north, with very high percentages of the LTU given their more or less average

*Table 18(a).   Age characteristics of the short- and long-term unemployed (STU, LTU) and the newly
                employed (NE), Spain, 1987 and 1990*

	Numbers (thousands)	%	Average age (years)	% under 22 years	% under 31% years	over 47 years
Males						
1987						
STU	631.1	100	31.2	28.5	60.8	16.5
LTU	977.9	100	32.2	24.5	59.5	19.5
NE	575.3	100	30.6	21.3	61.6	12.1
1990						
STU	604.1	100	32.0	24.2	57.6	16.5
LTU	560.2	100	33.8	28.9	53.6	21.2
NE	581.0	100	30.4	20.5	62.5	10.6
Females						
1987						
STU	367.4	100	26.5	39.2	76.1	5.6
LTU	935.2	100	27.0	35.9	74.5	6.0
NE	243.7	100	25.7	38.7	80.0	3.6
1990						
STU	486.2	100	28.4	29.4	67.1	7.0
LTU	767.7	100	29.5	21.3	64.7	7.3
NE	328.1	100	26.4	28.9	77.3	2.6

Source: *Labour Force Survey.*

unemployment rates. The latter regions represent an area of industrial decline where, it can be argued, a clear problem of the LTU exists. As for the former, it seems that the explanation has to do with the special characteristics of the production process in these regions (the agriculture-construction-tourism cycle), which generate a relatively high labour turnover. Here the problem is probably more of structural unemployment, rather than long-term unemployment; however, to the extent that it is always the same group of people who suffer the unemployment spells — no matter how brief — one can talk of a different kind of long-term unemployment problem. On the whole, however, with these important exceptions, our contention that the problem of the LTU is not different from the general problem of unemployment is borne out by the data.

Turning now to the comparison of the characteristics of the LTU, table 18 compares two different groups of unemployed defined by duration (less than one year and one year or more), the analysis being carried out separately for men and women. In addition, a third group has been added: those currently holding a job who declare that a year before they were unemployed. Thus, the LTU can be compared to two reference groups: their short-term counterparts and those who, like them, were unemployed one year before but who have managed to escape from that situation. Unfortunately, this latter comparison is somewhat hampered by the fact that no information is available on the unemployment situation of these leavers (most significantly, there is no information on past job experience, the time they

Table 18(b). Educational characteristics of the short- and long-term unemployed (STU, LTU) and the newly employed (NE), Spain, 1987 and 1990

	Average education level (years)	% with no education	% with at least secondary education	% students
Males				
1987				
STU	6.4	17.3	3.9	5.8
LTU	6.9	13.2	6.1	6.2
NE	6.8	12.9	5.0	1.7
1990				
STU	6.7	15.5	4.9	4.6
LTU	7.1	13.4	6.6	8.8
NE	7.0	12.3	4.1	1.3
Females				
1987				
STU	7.8	10.8	10.1	11.9
LTU	8.3	5.7	11.2	11.2
NE	8.3	7.2	12.8	3.3
1990				
STU	7.9	8.8	9.3	8.4
LTU	8.4	6.1	10.8	10.3
NE	9.0	4.5	15.5	3.8

Source: *Labour Force Survey.*

had been searching for work, the intensity of their search and whether or not they were beneficiaries of unemployment insurance schemes).

The analysis presented in table 18 is similar to that of table 15. First, in terms of age (table 18(a)), the newly employed (NE) tend to be younger than the short-term unemployed (STU) and the long-term unemployed (LTU), this being the case both for males and females and in 1987 as well as in 1990. All age indicators follow the same pattern with the exception of the proportion of youngsters aged under 22; this tends to be higher in the case of the STU than in the case of the NE.

As for years of schooling (table 18(b)), there appears to be no significant differences between men in the three groups. However, among women, the NE tend to have a higher average level of education, especially in 1990, and also a higher proportion of those with at least secondary education.

In terms of the position within the household (table 18(c)), there are no significant differences between the three groups, although being a non-household head where the head is unemployed seems to be less prevalent among the NE (excepting females in 1987). Similarly the presence of another unemployed family member is less common among the newly employed.

The conditions for accepting a prospective job (table 18(d)) do not seem to vary much between the STU and the LTU. In this case, the data for the NE are

Table 18(c). **Family characteristics of the short- and long-term unemployed (STU, LTU) and the newly employed (NE), Spain, 1987 and 1990**

	% household heads (HH)	% spouse of HH	% spouses of HH with unemployed HH	% children of HH	% children of HH with unemployed HH	% in household with no employed HH	In house-hold with at least one other unemployed
Males							
1987							
STU	38.9	0.5	0.2	54.0	6.4	45.2	37.6
LTU	35.4	0.6	0.1	57.8	6.4	40.6	41.9
NE	41.2	0.2	0.1	52.3	4.2	–	31.6
1990							
STU	39.4	0.3	0.1	54.5	5.2	44.0	34.9
LTU	38.6	0.6	0.2	54.2	3.5	41.2	34.7
NE	36.6	0.3	0.1	55.6	3.6	–	29.1
Females							
1987							
STU	4.3	29.2	6.9	60.5	5.5	26.1	39.2
LTU	3.6	27.1	4.0	64.3	6.3	25.3	38.7
NE	4.5	22.0	3.3	66.8	6.7	–	30.5
1990							
STU	4.7	36.4	6.0	54.7	4.4	23.7	30.3
LTU	5.5	35.3	4.5	55.1	3.9	23.1	30.4
NE	4.9	24.9	2.7	65.3	4.5	–	21.6

Source: *Labour Force Survey.*

not included because the relevant comparison would have to be the willingness of the newly employed at the time when they were unemployed (which is information not available from the *Labour Force Survey*).

Finally, table 18(e) gives four indicators relating to the unemployed with past job experience. These suggest that the LTU are more likely to have been made redundant while the STU are more likely to have come to the end of a contract. However, the differences tended to disappear between 1987 and 1990, perhaps due to the more widespread use of short-term contracts and to the corresponding increase in labour turnover. At the same time, the LTU tend to have stayed longer in their previous jobs than their short-term counterparts. We shall return to this result later on.

The two comparisons made in table 18, between short- and long-term unemployment and between the LTU and those who have managed to escape from that situation, could be made in a more sophisticated way by using discrete choice econometric models. Such models would aim to explain the probability of escaping from unemployment and the probability of becoming long-term unemployed. Unfortunately, as already mentioned, such modelling is hampered by the fact that we observe the unemployed *ex post* and not *ex ante*, as ideally we should.[11] Thus we have only estimated the first of the models, on escape from unemployment, which is the one least affected by these problems.[12]

Table 18(d). Job search characteristics of the short- and long-term unemployed (STU, LTU) and the newly employed (NE), Spain, 1987 and 1990

	% who would accept a job				% who would not accept a job			
	If it implied a change of residence	If it implied a change of occupation	With earnings lower than those corresponding to skill level	If it implied skill downgrading	If it implied a change of residence	If it implied a change of occupation	With earnings lower than those corresponding to skill level	If it implied skill downgrading
Males								
1987								
STU	44.8	75.9	63.5	71.8	35.8	12.3	18.7	12.7
LTU	42.1	74.9	66.2	71.4	36.0	11.7	14.9	11.5
1990								
STU	38.8	72.6	52.6	60.5	35.5	9.0	20.6	14.8
LTU	37.1	69.3	53.5	60.0	34.4	9.5	16.9	13.2
Females								
1987								
STU	27.6	74.1	64.3	70.4	55.1	12.4	16.2	13.1
LTU	26.3	72.4	61.3	66.0	53.7	12.0	16.9	13.8
1990								
STU	21.6	68.5	51.8	57.1	54.3	9.5	17.9	14.2
LTU	23.2	67.5	52.5	56.8	50.6	8.6	16.9	13.4

Source: Labour Force Survey.

Table 18(e).   Work experience characteristics of the short- and long-term unemployed (STU, LTU)
and the newly employed (NE), Spain, 1987 and 1990

	Who left their jobs because of end of contract	Who left their jobs because of dismissals	% less than one year in previous job	% more than three years in previous job
Males				
1987				
STU	62.5	23.3	64.3	16.3
LTU	47.4	37.5	45.2	31.8
1990				
LTU	76.4	10.7	67.7	11.0
STU	65.4	19.7	53.6	22.7
Females				
1987				
STU	61.6	19.8	65.2	12.5
LTU	46.7	30.0	47.3	24.2
1990				
STU	74.8	9.0	70.2	8.9
LTU	64.6	14.4	52.5	18.9

Source: *Labour Force Survey.*

We have fitted two "logit models" (one for males, one for females) comparing the characteristics of people who in 1990 (second quarter) declared that they had been in unemployment for at least 12 months with those who were in work but who were unemployed one year earlier.[13] By using these two groups, one is effectively explaining the probability of escaping from unemployment. The complete results of the model appear in the Appendix to this chapter. Figure 20 shows the estimated probabilities arising from the different values of the variables included.

The first general comment to be made is that escape probabilities for women are lower than those for men. Thus, the increasing feminization of unemployment in Spain can be attributed, at least partly, to the fact that women appear less able to escape from unemployment than men.

Age appears to be the most significant variable affecting the probability of escaping unemployment into employment. For males, this probability rises slightly up to 25-29 years and decreases quite dramatically afterwards. For females, the probabilities decrease steadily with age.

The position within the household also plays an important role. In particular, being a female spouse of the household head dramatically reduces the probability of escaping unemployment (the result also holds for male spouses but this group is insignificant). Taken together with other analyses not reported here (see Toharia, 1991), which suggest that unemployed female spouses tend to search for work less intensively than others, the question arises whether unemployed married women (around 35 per cent of total unemployment) really want to work. This is a difficult question to answer. The result could merely indicate that married

Figure 20.   Probabilities of "escaping" unemployment into employment, males and females, Spain, 1989-90

Probabilities (%)

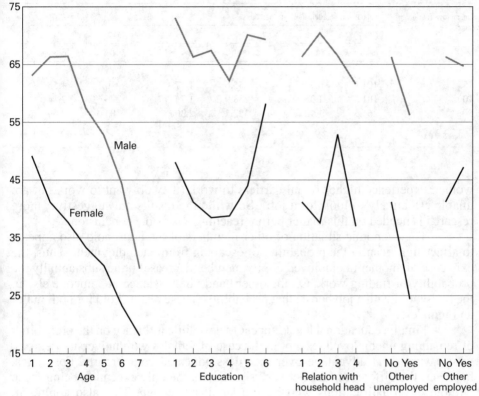

Key to variables (asterisks indicate the variable which remains constant when varying each of the others)

Age (years)
1. 16-19
2. 20-24 (*)
3. 25-29
4. 30-34
5. 35-39
6. 40-49
7. 50 and over

Education
1. Illiterates or without education
2. Primary education (*)
3. Lower secondary education
4. Upper secondary education
5. Vocational training
6. University-level education

Relation with household head
1. Household head (*)
2. Spouse
3. Child
4. Others

Other unemployed person
No. There is no other unemployed person in the household (*)
Yes. There is at least one other unemployed person in the household

Other employed person
No. There is no one employed in the household (*)
Yes. There is someone else employed in the household

Table 19. *Estimates of required new job creation on different unemployment and labour force*
participation assumptions, in Spain, 1990-2000; (yearly average employment creation,
thousands and per cent)

Unemployment rate target (%)	Labour-force participation rate in 2000					
	50%		52%		54%	
	(000)	(%)	(000)	(%)	(000)	(%)
15	101.2	0.78	155.6	1.17	210.1	1.55
10	181.3	1.35	238.9	1.75	296.6	2.14
5	261.3	1.90	322.2	2.30	383.0	2.69

Source: See text.

women experience higher social barriers to work (they do want to work but are unable effectively to look for a job). So while the results are suggestive, more research is needed on this matter before reaching a sensible conclusion.

The economic situation of other members of the household also appears to affect significantly the probability of escaping from unemployment. Thus, the existence of another unemployed family member decreases quite substantially the probability of finding work. On the other hand, the existence of someone else in the household with a job boosts that probability. These results hold for both males and females.

Finally, educational levels appear to have little influence on the probability of remaining unemployed, except in the case of females with university degrees, who have a clear advantage over their less educated counterparts. For males, however, the differences are not very significant, the only exception being those without any qualifications who have a small advantage. This also applies to females.[14]

The future prospects for unemployment

To conclude this chapter, we make some guesses as to the likely evolution of unemployment. This obviously depends on three factors, namely, population growth, participation rates and employment. Given population growth, which is fairly well known for the next 15 years (as all people entering the labour market 15 years from now are already born and mortality rates are quite easy to estimate), we make reasonable assumptions as to the behaviour of participation rates to get estimates of the labour force; we then set different unemployment targets and calculate the employment creation needed to meet them.

The results appear in table 19. The "baseline projection" for the year 2000 corresponds to a situation roughly equivalent to that existing in 1990: a participation rate of 50 per cent and an unemployment rate of 15 per cent. It implies that, merely to accommodate population growth, employment must increase by 1 million approximately over the 1990s. This figure increases as the target unemployment rate is lowered and as the estimated participation rate increases. Thus, for example, the "middle-range" estimate, corresponding to an unemployment target of 10 per cent and a participation rate of 52 per cent, implies an employment increase of 2.4 million over the next decade. If the unemployment target is lowered to 5 per cent and the participation rate is assumed to reach its 1976 level of 54 per cent, over 3.8 million new jobs would be needed to the year 2000, an employment creation rate faster than that observed in the 1985-91 period.

These calculations should be treated with care, since they are based on simple and aggregate assumptions. But they illustrate an important point: unemployment in Spain is likely to remain high for some time and rapid employment creation must be maintained to bring unemployment down. Needless to say, and as we have pointed out throughout this chapter, unemployment is far from having a homogeneous impact on different groups. The aggregate figures, therefore, provide only a first and very rough, albeit interesting, approximation.

Notes

[1] For clarity in the graphs, only these four dates will be considered from now on.

[2] The figures refer to the 15-19 group in 1964 and 1974 and to the 16-19 group in 1984 and 1989. Since 1980, youngsters under 16 are not legally allowed to work. Those doing compulsory military service have been excluded.

[3] The data come from specific analyses of the *Labour Force Survey* (*Encuesta de Población Activa*) tapes. This survey was reformed in 1987 to meet the standards of the European Labour Force Survey. The use of the second quarter data has the further advantage that, in that quarter, some retrospective questions on the situation of individuals a year earlier are included.

[4] This information about the family has been computed by taking advantage of the fact that the Labour Force Survey is a survey of households. We are grateful to Luis Garrido, who first had the idea of reconstructing households, as well as possessing the programming skills needed to do so.

[5] In this case, the information is restricted to those who had left their jobs in the previous 36 months. No information is collected for those having left their jobs earlier, to avoid problems of recollection.

[6] These latter figures do not follow directly from those in table 15(c), although they are obviously related to them. They come from the official results of the *Labour Force Survey*, which contain some information on households.

[7] As measured by a mismatch index suggested by Layard, Jackman and Savouri, 1990. This index is (half) the squared coefficient of variation of regional unemployment rates.

[8] That is, going from 2 to 10 per cent unemployment is not the same as going from 10 to 50 per cent or from 10 to 18 per cent.

[9] The 1981 and 1985 figures are yearly averages; the 1987 and 1990 figures correspond to the second quarter. All figures come from the *Labour Force Survey*. No attempt has been made to make the figures homogeneous since, for present purposes, this break in the series does not matter. A comparison between the earlier figures presented here and those estimated by Bentolila and Dolado (1990) to make them comparable to the post-1987 data shows no significant differences.

[10] The methodological change in the *Labour Force Survey* introduced in 1987 prevents comparisons with previous data: the way in which respondents were asked about search duration was changed from a ready-made scale question to an open-ended one, in which the number of months (up to 24) and years (thereafter) were asked. This change resulted in an increase in the proportion of LTU. One should thus be careful when comparing pre-1987 and post-1987 figures. We think it is best to avoid such a comparison altogether.

[11] The fact that only a sixth of the *Labour Force Survey* sample is renewed each quarter means that it is possible to follow up the unemployed at one point in time and study the evolution of their employment situation over six quarters. We would then have all the characteristics of the individuals

when they were unemployed *and* their characteristics one year later either as unemployed, employed or inactive. While this is technically feasible, and the Spanish Statistical Office is making efforts to make data available to external users, we have been unable to use them for this book, although we hope to be able to analyse them in the future.

[12] The problems here refer to lack of variables. In the comparison between the short-term and the long-term unemployed, more difficult conceptual issues are involved.

[13] We have eliminated from the analysis those declaring that they were currently studying.

[14] These differences in probabilities are related to labour demand and supply considerations which are the subject of following chapters.

Chapter 3

Wage flexibility

As we see it, flexibility refers to the ability of individuals in the economy, and notably in the labour market, to abandon established ways and adapt to new circumstances. (Dahrendorf et al., 1986, p. 6.)

Introduction

One of the main determinants of the macroeconomic performance of any country is the structure of the labour market. In particular, the degree of "flexibility" of this market is often claimed to be the key determinant of the evolution of unemployment. According to this view, there is a close relationship between high and persistent unemployment and excessive legal regulation of the labour market. In this and the following chapter, we examine whether this view is useful for explaining Spanish unemployment.

The first caveat which must be made relates to the definition of labour market flexibility, which is not only a multidimensional concept but also a very confusing one. There are many dimensions in which a labour market can be "flexible" or not, and the notion of "flexibility" means different things to different people. It could be possible that the labour market is not working efficiently but, then, it seems more productive to ask about the reasons and consequences of that lack of efficiency rather than to use labels which do not help to identify the basic problems.

The usual meaning of labour market flexibility, that is, the neoclassical sense, refers to the lack of labour market institutions that prevent the market reaching a continuous equilibrium, as determined by the intersection of the labour demand and the supply curves (Standing, 1989; for alternative definitions, see Toharia, 1988). A simple figure illustrates this definition (see figure 21). Suppose that the labour market is in equilibrium (at E_0 in the figure), the position given by the intersection of the labour demand curve, l_0^d, and the labour supply curve, l^s. Then, an external shock shifts the labour demand curve to the left (locus l_1^d). If the market were "perfectly flexible" the new equilibrium, given by the point E_1, would be reached immediately. The different degrees of labour market flexibility can be related to this illustrative example:

(i)   Employment flexibility is the absence of institutions constraining employment determination. If employment is determined by the intersection of the labour demand and supply curves, and if the labour market shows "perfect employment flexibility", the equilibrium level of employment (after a fall in labour productivity, as represented by the leftward shift in the labour demand curve in figure 21) would drop immediately (from E_0 to point A).

(ii) Similarly, wage flexibility, in general, refers to the absence of institutions constraining wage adjustments to changes in labour productivity. Thus, under the same assumption as in (i) regarding determination of labour market equilibrium, if labour productivity falls and wages are "perfectly flexible", they too would immediately drop (from E_0 to point B). The combination of different degrees of wage and employment flexibility determines which of the two variables, employment or real wages, is affected earlier in the adjustment process.

(iii) A third factor determining labour market flexibility is the duration of the adjustment process, that is, not the combination of wage and employment flexibility, but the magnitude of both types of flexibility. The greater the flexibility, the shorter the duration of the adjustment process and the less persistent the unemployment. Obviously, "perfect flexibility", of both employment and wages and in the neoclassical sense, would yield an instantaneous adjustment to changes in labour demand or labour supply conditions (that is, an instantaneous movement to point E_1 from point E_0).

(iv) Finally, micro-economic flexibility refers to the existence of several "local" labour markets, independent in the sense that the equilibrium in each market is determined by labour demand and supply in that market and not by the equilibrium in other markets, although this equilibrium could affect labour demand and supply in the latter. In other words, micro-economic flexibility refers to the speed and magnitude of sectoral wage and employment adjustments to changes in the *structure* of labour demand.

Both the definition and the desirability of labour market flexibility are much debated issues. Discussions about whether or not a labour market is flexible enough are not very productive, mainly because of the different degrees and dimensions of flexibility that have to be considered and because the concept of "flexibility" depends on the model of the labour market that we accept as valid for the analysis. For this reason, to identify the sources of "rigidities" or "inefficiencies" of the Spanish labour market, we start by presenting a theoretical model (after Layard and Nickell, 1986, and Blanchard, 1991, among others). Under this, it is possible to define precisely a degree of wage (in)flexibility and to make explicit the relationship between this concept and unemployment (see next section). This is followed by a description of the evolution of the relation between unemployment and inflation and that of the most relevant wage variables. Concretely, we analyse the evolution of average wages and wage differentials during the employment crisis period (1975-85) to assess the extent to which they were rigid and deserved blame for such a crisis. We also discuss the role played by incomes policies to moderate wage claims during that period. Subsequent sections present estimations of the above-mentioned model of the labour market

Figure 21.   An illustrative example of the neoclassical concept of labour market flexibility

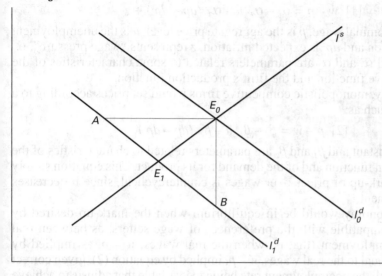

at several stages of its development and consider the legal framework affecting wage determination (which is mainly based on collective bargaining) to see if it is the source of wage rigidities. We conclude the chapter with some comments on the effects of EMU on the current system of collective bargaining.

Wage rigidity: Theoretical considerations and the relationship between rigidity and the equilibrium rate of unemployment

The determinants of wage rigidity and its relationship with unemployment obviously depend on the model accepted as a representation of the functioning of the labour market. For instance, in the pure neoclassical (perfect competition) model, wage flexibility is determined by the legal institutions constraining wage determination and, in more complicated versions, by the existence of job search costs which affect search intensity and, therefore, what is commonly known as "frictional" unemployment, that is, unemployment arising from people moving between jobs.

We adopt a different view of the labour market. We believe that both workers and firms have some degree of monopoly power and, therefore, some scope to set wages and prices, respectively. This is the view represented by the model developed by Layard and Nickell (1986), Layard, Nickell and Jackman (1991, Chapter 8) and Blanchard (1991). Thus, if we suppose a monopolistically competitive economy where wages are set by collective bargaining and use standard bargaining models (see Layard, Nickell and Jackman, 1991, Chapter 2) to represent this wage determination process, we would conclude that wages are determined according to an equation similar to the following:

$$[1] \quad w - p = \alpha_0 - \alpha_1 \, u - \alpha_2 \, (dp - dp^e) + z$$

where w is the nominal wage, p is the aggregate price level, u is the unemployment rate, dp is inflation and dp^e is expected inflation, z represents "wage pressure", α_0 is a constant and α_1 and α_2 are parameters related to some characteristics of the workers' objective function and the firm's production function.

Similarly, monopolistic competitive firms would set prices according to a price equation such as:[1]

$$[2] \quad p - w = \beta_0 - \beta_1 \, u - \beta_2 \, (dp - dp^e)$$

where β_0 is a constant and β_1 and β_2 are parameters related to characteristics of the firm's production function and of the demand for its product. This equation simply says that the mark-up of prices over wages is countercyclical, since it decreases with unemployment.[2]

This economy would be in equilibrium when the mark-up desired by employers is compatible with the preferences of wage setters, as between real wages and unemployment (that is, when the real wages, $w - p$, as implied by equation (1) is equal to the real wages, $w - p$, implied by equation (2), given correct expectations, with the unemployment rate being the variable that adjusts to achieve equilibrium (see figure 22)). In this case, the equilibrium unemployment rate, which is also a "natural rate" and the Non-Accelerating Inflation Rate of Unemployment (NAIRU, henceforth) under some conditions (see Layard, Nickell and Jackman, 1991, Chapter 8), is given by:[3]

$$[3] \quad u^* = \frac{\alpha_0 + \beta_0 + z}{\alpha_1 + \beta_1}$$

Thus, we can define an index of real wage rigidity by $(\alpha_1 + \beta_1)^{-1}$, that is, the increase in equilibrium unemployment needed to accommodate a unit increase in "wage pressure" at constant inflation (that is, when $dp = dp^e$). Similarly, we can take the coefficient $(\alpha_2 + \beta_2)(\alpha_1 + \beta_1)^{-1}$ as an index of nominal wage rigidity, since it represents the amount of unemployment needed to reduce inflation by one percentage point.[4] It is obvious that the greater the real wage rigidity the higher the equilibrium rate of unemployment.

Unemployment-inflation trade-offs and the equilibrium unemployment rate

How can we know if the equilibrium unemployment rate is high or low, increasing or decreasing? As this concept cannot be observed directly, we must choose between two alternatives. The first one is obvious: estimation of the parameters of the model above (we will comment on the available estimations of the Spanish equilibrium unemployment rate below). The second alternative is to look at the joint evolution of inflation and unemployment and infer from it the

Figure 22.   The equilibrium unemployment rate: (1) wage equation, (2) price equation

w-p

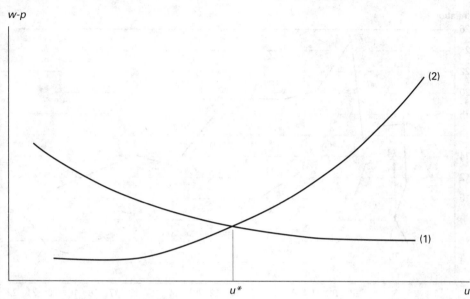

u*   *u*

evolution of such an unemployment rate. This is what we attempt to do in this section.

As we have already noted, one of the features of Spanish unemployment in recent years is its persistence despite the rise in employment (a persistence which is mainly due, as we saw in Chapter 2, to increases in participation rates). A related observation refers to the diminishing deflationary effects of unemployment, and this signals a rise in the equilibrium unemployment rate (the NAIRU). Recent studies show that in most OECD countries the NAIRU has increased, simultaneously with the actual unemployment rate, during the 1970s and early 1980s (see the various papers in the special 1986 issue of *Economica*). Spain is no exception. Some authors claim that the *equilibrium* unemployment rate in Spain is, in common with the *actual* unemployment rate, among the highest in western countries (Dolado, Malo de Molina and Zabalza, 1986; Andrés et al., 1991; and Lamo and Dolado, 1991).

Figure 23 presents the inflation-unemployment locus in Spain and in the EC as a whole (with a pattern which is very similar across member countries). There are several differences between them. First, inflation in Spain increased until 1977, while in the EC it stopped increasing in 1974. While in the EC monetary policy did not accommodate the price increases resulting from the first oil shock and the wage pressures existing since the late 1960s, Spanish governments pursued accommodating monetary policies until 1978 when the "Moncloa Pacts" were reached. After the second oil price shock in 1979, inflation increased in the EC countries but not in Spain, mainly because of the policy of wage restraint adopted by Spanish unions at that time. The post-1980 disinflationary process was achieved both in Spain and in the EC at a substantial cost in terms of unemployment;

Figure 23.   Unemployment and inflation in Spain and the EC, 1970-89

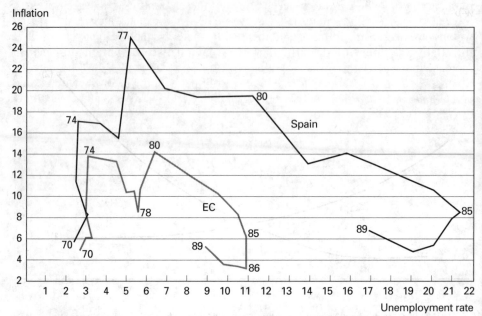

Note: The unemployment rate is the OECD standardized unemployment rate (from *Historical Statistics*, Paris, 1990). The inflation rate is the annual change in the consumer price index (same source).

however, the process was much more intense in Spain possibly because its starting inflation levels were higher. In the second half of the 1980s, after the (favourable) third oil shock in 1985, unemployment started to fall in Spain and in the EC; this time around, however, deflation continued in Spain until 1988 while in the Community inflationary pressures began to build up as soon as unemployment began its decline.

These loci also illustrate the behaviour of the NAIRU. If we add up the wage and price equation presented above we get an expectations-augmented Philips curve (very common in the analysis of the determination of inflation):

$$[4] \quad \pi = \pi^e + \lambda \, (u - u^*) + z$$

where π is the inflation rate, π^e is expected inflation (or "core" inflation), u is the unemployment rate, u^* is the NAIRU and z are supply shocks (raw materials price increases and wage shocks) which we have included for completeness. The fact that unemployment increases even when inflation does not decline implies, according to this type of equation, that either core inflation is lower than the actual rate of inflation, or that the NAIRU is higher than the actual unemployment rate, or that there are some adverse supply shocks ($z > 0$) at work. While it is difficult to distinguish which of these three factors shift the inflation-unemployment trade-off locus, an attempt can be made to identify changes in the NAIRU from the above. For instance, while the evolution of inflation after the first two oil shocks is closely related to the first and third factors (transitory increase in "core" inflation and supply shocks), it is difficult to find explanations for the 1981-86 period (when monetary policy was contractionary in most of these countries, wage pressure was low and the prices of raw materials were more or less constant). During this period we observe decreasing inflation and increasing unemployment. However, the drop in inflation is rather mild, particularly in Spain. This observation suggests an increase in the NAIRU. Dolado, Malo de Molina and Zabalza (1986) estimate the Spanish NAIRU at 7 per cent for 1973-79 and 11 per cent for 1980-84, while Lamo and Dolado estimates the NAIRU at 15 per cent for 1985-90. We shall present more estimations of this type below.

The determinants of wage rigidity

The next question that must be answered refers to the variables which determine the main parameters of the model and, therefore, nominal and real wage rigidity and the equilibrium unemployment rate. At this point, it is helpful to look at figure 22 and ask about the determinants of the position of the wage and price curves. First, capital accumulation and the degree of competition in the product market determine the position of the price curve (the inverse of the labour demand curve, that is, the level of employment that firms will demand at each real wage). Second, the characteristics of collective bargaining between workers and employers and, more concretely, the workers' bargaining power determine the relationship between target real wages and employment from the workers' perspective. In particular, increases in wage targets (unwarranted by labour productivity growth) push up the equilibrium rate of unemployment.[5] Finally, wage targets and, more generally, the results of collective bargaining will be affected by the influence that the unemployed can exercise on wage negotiators.

So far, we have excluded from this discussion "hysteresis effects" in both wage and price setting. To the extent that "hysteresis effects" exist, there will be a difference between short-run and long-run equilibrium unemployment rates, the short-run rate being a linear combination of the long-run rate and past unemployment. "Hysteresis effects" in wage setting arise when not only current unemployment but also past unemployment affect the workers' target real wage. This can happen either when there are "insider effects" or when the influence of the unemployed on the wage determination process is decreasing with unemployment duration, due, for instance, to detachment of the labour force or lack of skills. We now review the role played by each of these determinants of wage rigidity and the equilibrium unemployment rate and of the sources of "hysteresis", in relation to the Spanish economy.[6]

A. Capital accumulation and the unemployment rate

The importance of this factor as a determinant of the equilibrium unemployment rate and as a source of hysteresis was originally pointed out by Bruno and Sachs (1985). During a recession, unemployment rises and, possibly, net investment turns negative. If that is the case, the capital stock decreases which implies a further increase in current and future unemployment. During the employment crisis, the capital stock of the Spanish economy declined sharply, contributing to the increase in unemployment in the early 1980s, but capital accumulation recovered very quickly since 1984 and has not subsequently been an important constraint on employment creation.

B. Mismatch between labour supply and labour demand

In a purely competitive labour market, mismatch can be the consequence of an inefficient matching system and of insufficient search activity. Obviously, the greater the extent of mismatch, the higher the equilibrium unemployment rate. For our non-competitive model of the labour market, the existence of mismatch is also important since it affects wage-setting behaviour. If there is mismatch, there could be wage pressure in some sectors or regions independent of the average level of unemployment (see Layard, Nickell and Jackman, 1991, Chapter 5). There are several procedures to assess the degree of mismatch between labour demand and supply. Under several assumptions (see Layard, Jackman and Savouri, 1990), unemployment rate dispersion (geographical and sectoral) is a measure of mismatch. Alternatively, in a multisectoral disequilibrium model with different sectors facing different constraints, that is, shortage of effective demand, productive capacity or labour (see Drèze, 1990), mismatch is identified with the disparity of this shortage across sectors. Finally, a less theoretical and more pragmatic way to examine the degree of mismatch is to analyse the distribution of employment and the changes in this distribution as indicative of the duration of situations of excess demand or supply of labour of particular sectors or regions.

Bentolila and Dolado (1990) present some evidence on the first two measures of mismatch. Significantly, unemployment dispersion (by regions or sectors) in Spain is not higher than in other European countries (see Layard, Nickell and Jackman, 1991), and has remained stable or steadily decreased — depending on the categories considered — since 1977 or earlier. Bentolila and Dolado also compute the disequilibrium version of the mismatch index and find that this measure follows a similar path to that of the unemployment rate. They conclude that this second measure is indicative of a high degree of mismatch in the Spanish labour market which can explain part of the increase in the equilibrium unemployment rate. Nevertheless, the increase in employment and the huge turnover observed in the Spanish labour market suggest that employers find the workers that they need to fill their job vacancies without much difficulty. Thus, although there may be some mismatch between labour demand and supply in some specific occupations, it may also be possible that its importance is being overemphasized.

C. Labour mobility

Labour mobility can be an important factor determining the level of the equilibrium unemployment rate if unemployed workers do exert some influence on wage determination. Additionally, it can contribute to the solution of transitory mismatch problems. However, a *vicious circle* links labour mobility and the functioning of the labour market. In a depressed labour market, the unemployed may become discouraged or accustomed to their situation and stop searching for a job. Hence, they cease to exert influence in the process which determines wages and employment levels. As a consequence, "insiders" bargain for higher wages and employment creation is low. This discourages labour mobility since there is no point in moving when there are no jobs to move to.

Bentolila and Dolado (1990) have analysed migration flows in Spain since 1962. They consider migration flows as the result of risk-neutral people moving where their human capital is more valuable (that is, where wages and employment probabilities are higher). They found that these flows react to real wage and unemployment differentials across regions but with small elasticities and long lags. That is, there is some evidence that these flows are related to the situation in regional labour markets, which imply, among other things, that high (low) unemployment in the destination region discourages (encourages) migration into that region. On this view, the unemployment protection can also be blamed for such low labour mobility. However, they failed to identify a significant effect of labour mobility on employment creation or real wages. This suggests that the characteristics of collective bargaining in Spain include strong "insider" effects that play a more important role in wage setting than the effects of migrant "outsiders".

Alternatively, one can think that people are risk-averse and, thus, that the more important restriction to labour mobility is the matching process between the unemployed in one region and vacancies in another (see Jackman and Savouri, 1990). In this case, the low labour mobility observed in Spain can be attributed to the high degree of inefficiency of public employment agencies (and the limited role played by private employment agencies), an issue to which we will return in Chapter 5. Unfortunately, there are not enough data to allow us to assess which view of labour mobility (the "human capital" or the "matching") is more accurate, but there are reasons to believe that the inefficiency of the "matching" system in the Spanish labour market may be playing a greater role than is generally recognized in keeping labour mobility so low.

D. The composition of unemployment by duration

There are two reasons why the duration of unemployment affects wage rigidity and the equilibrium unemployment rate. First, firms may be reluctant (with or without justified reasons) to hire long-term unemployed people. In this case, "insiders" have a greater incentive to pursue higher wage claims, the higher the proportion of long-term unemployment. Secondly, there is some relationship between long-term unemployment, mismatch and labour mobility. If the long-term unemployed lose skills and/or become accustomed to their position (perhaps because of generous unemployment benefits), then they will not search intensively for a job, so that mismatch increases and labour mobility decreases.

In the Spanish case, the proportion of long-term unemployment is quite high but is mainly concentrated among youngsters and second earners within the household (see Chapter 2). Unemployment benefits are generous, but are (more or less) limited in time and restricted to unemployed workers with previous jobs (see

Chapter 5). Thus, it is dubious that the unemployment benefit system is the main cause of long-term unemployment, as may be the case in other Western European countries (see Burda, 1988). In fact, male long-term unemployment decreased considerably during the 1985-90 period, in contrast to what happened in most other OECD countries (as we saw in Chapter 2).

E. Collective bargaining and the role of the unions

As noted above, the system of wage bargaining is a critical element in determining the equilibrium unemployment rate, because the scope for the existence of "insider" effects in wage setting arises mainly from the characteristics of such a system. It is well-known that in countries where there is centralized bargaining — such as Austria, Sweden or Germany — the employment level is higher and the unemployment rate lower than in countries where collective bargaining is decentralized (see Calmfors and Driffill, 1988).[7] There are several reasons for this (see Jimeno, 1991b). In particular, decentralized bargaining allows workers in different sectors to try to improve their relative situation. As a consequence, the resulting equilibrium unemployment rate is higher than for a centralized system where bargaining over relative wages is not possible.

Centralization is another concept over which some confusion exists. The first component of this concept is the level at which wage setting takes place (national level, industry or firm). But there are other characteristics of the wage setting process that also affect the degree of centralization of such a process, independently of the level at which negotiations take place. These two elements are coordination among employers and among trade unions and synchronization of the negotiations. Thus, to assess the degree to which a certain collective bargaining system is centralized, one must consider not only the level of negotiations but also coordination and synchronization. We will do this for Spanish collective bargaining below. As will be made clear, the number of collective bargaining units is excessive since negotiations at the industrial level and the firm level overlap. Furthermore, the degree of coordination among bargaining units is not excessively high, despite the fact that the two majority trade union confederations (UGT and CC.OO.) are coordinated to some extent, except for occasional breakdowns. But, on the other hand, the coordination among employers is more questionable. Finally, synchronization is low, as wage setting takes place throughout the year (with some concentration between March and August of each year) and most collective agreements are revised annually. As a result, the degree of centralization of collective bargaining in Spain is, currently, moderately decentralized.

F. Specific factors affecting the evolution of the Spanish NAIRU

Besides the general factors described above, more specific ones can be cited to explain the increase in the Spanish NAIRU. The empirical work by Dolado et al. (1986) and by Andrés et al. (1991) suggests the following:

(i) The increase in the "wage wedge" — the difference between the cost to the firm of employing a worker and the wage (net of taxes) that the worker receives — due mainly to increases in direct taxation and in employers' contributions to social security.

(ii) The unemployment protection system. Replacement ratios are not excessive. But the composition of unemployment, combined with some characteristics of the Spanish unemployment protection system (described in Chapter 5) may have resulted in low incentives for the unemployed to take available jobs, and this can create long-term unemployment and, plausibly, "hysteresis effects".

(iii) High inflation in the non-tradeable sector of the economy, which translates into wage pressure in the tradeable sector and, given the characteristics of Spanish collective bargaining, into wage increases across all sectors.

(iv) Finally, the huge increase of fixed-term employment (see Chapter 4) which may have increased segmentation of the labour market and conferred greater bargaining power on "insiders" (as argued by Jimeno and Toharia, 1991b). We will consider more deeply the wage effects of fixed-term employment in Chapter 4.

Wages and the employment crisis (1975-85)

Wage rigidity has been blamed as one of the main causes of the increase in unemployment during the period of employment crisis in the Spanish economy. We now discuss to what extent the evolution of wages show such rigidity. Before discussing this issue, it should be noted that explanations of unemployment based on the behaviour of real wages are doomed to failure for purely theoretical reasons. In any reasonable model of the labour market, (un)employment and real wages are endogenous variables determined simultaneously, and who is to say which variable is the cause and which is the result (as argued by Solow, 1986, Layard and Nickell, 1986, and Blanchard, 1991, among others; and as is obvious from the structure of the model sketched earlier).

In examining the relationship between wages and unemployment, we must distinguish between the average wage rate and the wage structure. Wages started to grow rapidly in the early 1970s. At the same time, wage dispersion showed some tendency to become excessively compressed (both in terms of industrial and occupational differentials). Average real wages have increased significantly in Spain ever since the 1960s. This increase, and, in particular, the wage explosion of 1973-77, paralleled the beginning of the period of big employment losses. However, any conclusion on the employment impact of the increase in wages must take the following points into account:

(i) The actual magnitude of the increase in wages is uncertain. Figures 24 and 25 present the evolution of wage rates and earnings in manufacturing and of the wage share in GDP. It should be noted that information on the evolution of actual wages is mainly based on the Statistical Office's earnings survey, which has a limited coverage and,

Figure 24.   Wage increases in manufacturing in Spain and other western countries, 1978-85

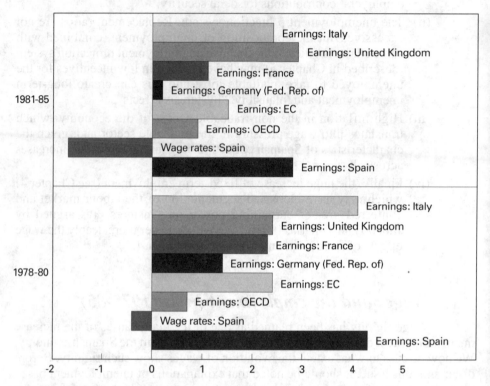

Notes: (i) Earnings increases are annual averages of real hourly earnings in manufacturing from OECD, *Historical Statistics*, Paris, 1990. (ii) Wage rate increases in Spain are annual averages in real terms computed as the difference between nominal wage rate increases (from *Estadísticas de Convenios Colectivos*, Ministry of Employment, various years) and actual inflation (measured by changes in the cost-of-living index).

until recently, suffered from a series of technical problems, which gave an upward bias to its estimates of wage increases (Lorente, 1982, 1986 and 1987). The data on which figure 25 is based come from the national accounts, but they may also suffer from the same upward bias since they use the earnings survey as an information source. In any case, it is difficult to find evidence of "excessive" real wage increases after 1978. Throughout the period since then, real wage rates have fallen, since inflation has usually been higher than nominal wage rate increases resulting from collective bargaining. Real hourly earnings in manufacturing have moderated their growth after 1980. It could be argued that non-wage labour costs were the most important factor in the evolution of labour costs. For example, Bentolila and Blanchard (1990) review wage regressions where non-wage labour costs are significant. However, while these non-wage labour costs (measured as the proportion of social security contributions in total employee

Figure 25. *Evolution of wage share in GDP, unadjusted and adjusted for the changing proportion of wage and salary earners, Spain, 1970-84*

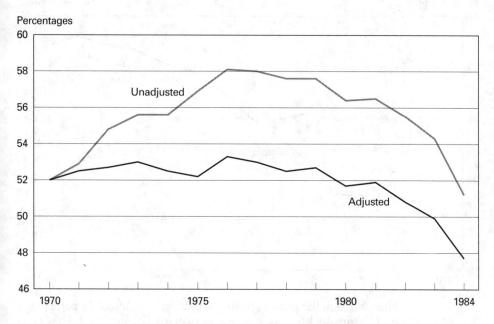

compensation) did increase significantly over the crisis period (see figure 26), they are already included in the wage index calculated from the national accounts, which represents total gross employee compensation (i.e. including social security contributions).

(ii) The increase in wages did not lead to a profit squeeze. Instead, businesses were able to raise their prices to make up for these increases or absorbed them through increases in productivity (Toharia, 1986). As figure 28 shows, unit labour costs (i.e. the ratio of average wage per worker to average labour productivity) remained virtually stable (with the only notable exception being 1976, the first year after Franco's death) throughout the period under consideration. This implies that the increase of more than 6 percentage points in the wage share between 1970 and 1976 (see figure 26) can be attributed almost entirely to the increased proportion of wage-earners in total employment. If this proportion is kept constant, then the change in the wage share between these two years barely exceeds 1 percentage point. Moreover, there was no wage-led profit squeeze in important subsectors of the economy, such as manufacturing, over the 1970-84 period. Some authors have published alarming figures, based on questionable handling of data that are by no means problem-free. But other recent estimates reveal very moderate declines in business profits due to wage increases. For example, Malo de Molina and Ortega (1984) estimated that the share of gross operating profits in

Figure 26.   Non-wage labour costs as a proportion of total employee compensation, Spain, 1970-84

value added in the manufacturing sector fell by almost 28 percentage points, from 44.1 to 16.4 per cent, between 1970 and 1984. However, publication of the 1980 input-output tables allowed others to estimate, on more reliable data, that the drop could not have been more than 4 percentage points (Albarracín, 1986). This does not imply that profits remained stable. The scarce available evidence suggests that profit rates did fall sharply in 1975-76, only to recover slightly thereafter. The main cause of the decline, however, was not the evolution of wages, as the data in figure 28 bear out, but rather the drastic changes in demand conditions as well as the prices of other inputs, especially energy (Toharia, 1981, 1987).

(iii) It is true that part of the productivity increases that allowed firms to keep down unit labour costs could have been induced by wage increases leading to the substitution of labour for capital, both in the product market through the demise of labour-intensive firms, and within the remaining firms (through reorganization). We believe, however, that the increases in productivity had less to do with labour shedding through closure of the most inefficient units, and more to do with company reorganizations and technical progress. Technical change has had a significant impact on the decline of employment, according to recent studies (Jaumandreu, 1986, and Segura and Jaumandreu, 1987). The question remains as to what extent this far-reaching reorganization, whatever its origin, was an essential prerequisite for most Spanish firms to be able to compete effectively internationally and in the more difficult markets created by the crisis.

Figure 27.   Evolution of real wages and unit labour costs, Spain, 1970-87

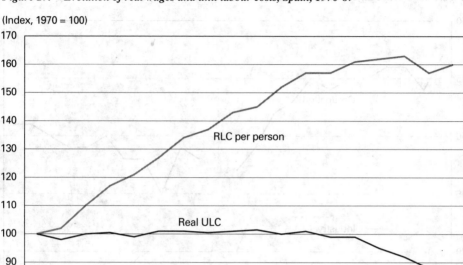

(Index, 1970 = 100)

Notes: RLC (Real Labour Cost) per person is the total wage bill, deflated by the GDP deflator, divided by the number of waged and salaried workers: Real ULC (Unit Labour Costs) is RLC per person divided by average productivity per employed person.

(iv) The majority of studies that primarily blame wages for increased unemployment do not take account of the radical change in both the objectives and results of the wage policy adopted since the advent of democracy in 1977 and, more importantly, the "social pacts" initiated in 1978 — in the so-called "Moncloa Pacts" — and consolidated in 1980 (see next section). The labour organizations adhered to this policy, a dramatic departure from their initial positions after Franco's death. As a consequence, Spain has been one of the few OECD countries to register a steady decline in real wage rates and unit labour costs, as figures 25 and 28 clearly show.

(v) Finally, from empirical studies we know that the short-run elasticity of employment with respect to labour costs in the Spanish economy is not large, at about 0.2-0.3, while the corresponding long-run elasticity seems to be close to one (Dolado, 1991). With these elasticities, it is difficult to explain the rapidity and magnitude by which employment fell.

Although information on wage differentials is scarce and barely adequate (see figure 29 for the available data), it suggests that the occupational wage structure narrowed fairly consistently until 1979 and increased subsequently. Inter-industry wage differentials declined sharply from 1975 to 1980, and then started to widen again.

Figure 28.   Wage differentials by industry and occupation, Spain, 1965-87

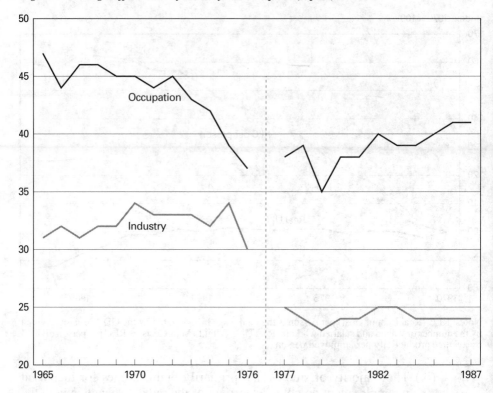

Notes: Coefficient of variation calculated as the unweighted standard deviation divided by unweighted mean earnings, expressed as a percentage. Data before and after 1977 are not comparable due to methodological changes of the earnings survey.

   The decline in occupational wage differentials would seem to have been largely brought about by the practice of demanding lump sum, rather than proportional, wage increases. This became widespread in the highly inflationary environment of the last years of the Franco regime and was recognized in the wage guidelines for 1979, which recommended that part of the increase be distributed as a fixed amount, for each worker. However, from 1979, the extremely regressive system of withholding taxes was replaced by a moderately progressive income tax. This made it easier to change the wage policy, which was coming under attack from high wage-earners. The subsequent negotiation of proportional wage increases — the same for all occupational groups — obviously implied an increase in wage differentials.

   Regarding inter-industry wage differentials, a hypothesis has already been advanced to explain their widening during the boom years: the pronounced narrowing of those differentials in the mid-1970s could be interpreted as the result of accumulated grievances created by the earlier widening, and happened even though the lowest-wage industries had the weakest productive structures and were hardest hit by job losses. However, the drop in employment, together with the centralized wage policy pursued from 1980 on, put an end to the narrowing of inter-industry wage differentials.

The relationship between the evolution of differentials and the loss of employment is fairly obvious. The most inefficient firms were no longer able to pay the higher wages and this, together with other factors such as tax reform and the prospect of increased international competition, hastened their demise. In addition, given the overmanning of most firms (especially with respect to unskilled workers) encouraged by the system of labour relations during the Franco era, the narrowing of occupational wage differentials meant that firms had to adjust not only the magnitude but also the structure of their workforce by reducing the number of unskilled workers. Bearing in mind the characteristics of the employment loss, it would seem that this factor goes further towards explaining employment reductions than the evolution of the average wage level.

The concept of micro-economic flexibility is also related to wage differentials, since it refers to the adjustment of sectoral wages to sectoral changes in labour productivity. As defined in the introduction to this chapter, the labour market is said to be micro-economically flexible when wages adjust to the sectoral dispersion in labour productivity, avoiding adjustment through employment. There are two factors that determine the degree of this type of flexibility: the extent of centralization of collective bargaining and whether outcomes at higher levels of negotiation are imposed further down; and the magnitude and dispersion across firms of wage drift (the difference between actual wages and wage rates) that might undo the influence of centralized bargaining.

The succession of nationwide agreements between the Government and major union and employer confederations of the late 1970s and early 1980s (see next section) supposedly adversely affected micro-economic flexibility. The reasons for this are well-known and already noted: the narrow range of wage-rate increases contained in those agreements did not allow for further wage adjustments to accommodate special circumstances. It is not surprising, as table 20 shows, that the sectoral dispersion of wages was also very low. It is more surprising that since 1986, when there has been no economy-wide agreement, this dispersion has not increased significantly, despite the high degree of decentralization of collective bargaining. This suggests that the blame for "micro-economic inefficiency", if there is any, should not be put on these nationwide agreements.

On the other hand, whether micro-economic flexibility is a desirable outcome is debatable. Some authors argue that wages and labour productivity should move together in each sector, that is, sectors with low (high) productivity growth should experience low (high) wage growth. An opposite view is that a low sectoral dispersion of wages is desirable, so that employment moves from sectors with low productivity growth to sectors with high productivity growth (Salter, 1966). In fact, as Jimeno (1991b) shows, provided there are no non-linearities in the relationship between wages and labour productivity or dynamic effects from productivity growth, these two proposals have similar effects on aggregate employment. Obviously, the most beneficial situation in terms of employment is an asymmetry in the evolution of wages and productivity, so that low productivity

Table 20.   Wage rate increases agreed in collective bargaining, and industry dispersion, Spain, 1983-89

	1983	1984	1985	1986	1987	1988	1989 [1]
All agreements (44 sectors)							
Wage increase	11.44	7.81	7.90	8.23	6.51	6.38	6.68
Standard deviation	0.90	0.87	0.58	0.47	0.94	0.75	0.69
Industry level (38 sectors)							
Wage increase	11.39	7.97	7.93	8.23	6.55	6.50	6.74
Standard deviation	1.30	0.83	0.80	0.71	1.21	0.95	0.83
Firm level (43 Sectors)							
Wage increase	11.66	7.02	7.75	8.23	6.33	5.69	6.37
Standard deviation	0.94	0.79	0.78	0.42	0.51	0.95	0.67

[1] Provisional.
Note: The standard deviation reported in the table is unweighted.
Source: Computed from Ministerio de Trabajo y Seguridad Social, *Boletín de Estadísticas Laborales*, various issues.

sectors experience low growth of labour costs and high productivity sectors experience moderate growth of labour costs. This would encourage employment in the latter without destroying jobs in the former. Jimeno (1987) presents some evidence on the micro-economic flexibility of labour costs in Spanish industry and finds evidence of this type of asymmetry.

There is a final issue with respect to both average wages and wages differentials: to what extent should or could trends be reversed? It should be stressed that in recent years there have been a number of changes stemming from major shifts of attitude by trade unions as well as their concern about unemployment. Whether or not even greater changes might take place in the future depends on how the economy evolves. Wage costs, however, have already shown a sizeable decline, while wage dispersion, which has remained fairly stable in the last few years — even widening a little in terms of occupational differentials — is still among the highest in Europe (see some recent data regarding Spain in table 21). It is also clear that many of the processes described above are deeply rooted in the new social situation and would, thus, be difficult to change. After all, the evolution of wages in Spain between 1975 and 1978 is almost a textbook example of the effects of unionization: a once-for-all jump in the absolute levels of real wages and a "standardization" or normalization of wages effectively establishing the principle of "equal pay for equal work".

The influence of incomes policies

As we saw in Chapter 1, one of the main problems that the Spanish economy had to face in the mid-1970s was an inflation shock. Inflationary pressure started to build up in the late 1960s and became more marked in the early 1970s, reinforced by the first oil shock. The policy response at that time consisted of an

Table 21. Yearly earnings (thousands of pesetas), Spain, 1988

Occupations	Total			Permanent contracts			Fixed-term contracts		
	Total	Male	Female	Total	Male	Female	Total	Male	Female
Total	1 587	1 672	1 236	1 803	1 887	1 419	1 040	1 089	877
1. Engineers and professionals	3 561	3 636	2 626	3 653	3 714	2 775	2 406	2 509	1 946
2. Technical staff	2 746	2 813	2 024	2 894	2 949	2 216	1 842	1 913	1 433
3. Managers, etc.	2 551	2 584	2 221	2 615	2 643	2 310	1 559	1 680	1 445
4. Assistants, etc.	2 033	2 085	1 578	2 140	2 174	1 768	1 328	1 388	1 123
5. Senior clerical workers	1 815	1 896	1 633	1 888	1 964	1 713	1 254	1 323	1 135
6. Subordinate clerical workers	1 565	1 610	1 396	1 672	1 707	1 526	1 052	1 079	984
7. Junior clerical workers	1 173	1 263	1 092	1 303	1 398	1 209	969	1 021	930
8. Senior skilled workers	1 445	1 474	1 117	1 560	1 590	1 212	1 131	1 155	902
9. Junior skilled workers	1 302	1 364	1 068	1 427	1 495	1 168	1 018	1 065	853
10. Production workers (labourers)	958	994	842	1 081	1 118	986	886	928	731
11.-12. Workers aged 16-18	602	628	548	786	806	730	582	607	533

Source: Instituto Nacional de Estadística (1992): *La distribución salarial en España*, Madrid.

accommodating monetary policy and a loose fiscal policy. In addition, since wages were indexed to past inflation (a peculiarity of the system of collective bargaining in which government intervention was widespread), a wage-price inflationary spiral was put in place. In 1977, and within the context of political reform (legalization of political parties and free elections), the Government proposed a national agreement to ease the transition to a democratic regime and to improve the economic situation. This agreement is known as the "Moncloa Pacts". Even without the formal participation of employer associations or trade unions (which were still not legalized), the pacts included national guidelines for wage setting and a recommendation that wage increases be determined according to expected and not past inflation. They were successful in reducing inflation and, more importantly, created the environment needed for the development of some aspects of corporatism or, at least, "social partnership" that resulted in subsequent national agreements. As we shall see later on, these aspects of corporatism have not been a permanent feature of the labour relations system.

However, after the "Moncloa Pacts" and during the early 1980s, there were continued attempts to achieve some degree of corporatism in the Spanish economy. Other economy-wide agreements were reached between employer associations, some trade unions and even on occasion the Government (see table 22). The typical national agreement between government, employer associations and unions had two parts:

(i)   a government declaration on the objectives of economic policy, a set of economic forecasts and tripartite agreements on incomes policies, social security, unemployment protection, generic employment conditions, training and wage increases for workers in public administration; and

(ii) an agreement between the employer associations and the trade unions, the main element of which was the band of permitted wage increase but which also contained agreements on other employment conditions, such as productivity increases and worker absenteeism, design of the collective bargaining structure and conflict resolution.

Spanish governments, sometimes in a weak position (in the 1978-82 period), sometimes for political convenience (the socialist government in 1984), and always under pressure because of the unemployment problem, have agreed to negotiate on the first set of issues with unions and employers. As a condition, they promoted economy-wide agreements covering the second set of issues. Their interest in these agreements was to reduce the conflict associated with the creation of a new system of labour relations. However, as table 21 shows, not all unions signed all of these agreements. In particular, the communist trade union confederation, Comisiones Obreras (CC.OO.), has traditionally opposed such agreements. It is important to note that the outcome of these negotiations is binding only for the signatories. The agreements do not bind other employer or worker associations or those participating in collective bargaining at lower levels. Even though their influence on social and economic policy has gone beyond wage determination (the agreements have proposed several modifications to the legal

Table 22. Economy-wide agreements and inflation in Spain, 1978-90

	Signing parties	Increase in wage rate: range (%)	Projected duration	Actual wage rate increase [1] (%)	Inflation [2] (%)
1978 Moncloa Pacts	Political parties	20-22	Free	20.6	19.8
1979 No agreement	Decree law	11-14	Free	14.1	15.7
1980 *Acuerdo Marco Interconfederal (AMI)*	UGT, CEOE	13-16	2 years (recommended)	15.3	15.6
1981 EXTENSION AMI	UGT, CEOE	11-15	Free (1 Year)	13.1	14.6
1982 *Acuerdo Nacional de Empleo (ANE)*	CC.OO., UGT, CEOE	9-11	Free (1 year)	12.0	14.4
1983 *Acuerdo Interconfederal (AI)*	CC.OO., UGT, CEOE	9.5-12.5	More than 1 year (if possible)	11.4	12.2
1984 No agreement	–	–	–	7.8	11.3
1985 *Acuerdo Económico y Social (AES)* — 1st Year	UGT, CEOE, Government	5.5-7.5	2 years (recommended)	7.9	8.8
1986 AES — 2nd year	UGT, CEOE, Government	7.2-8.6	2 years (recommended)	8.2	8.8
1987 No agreement	–	–	–	6.5	5.3
1988 No agreement	–	–	–	6.3	4.8
1989 No agreement	–	–	–	6.7	6.8
1990 No agreement	–	–	–	8.3	6.5

Notes: The UGT and the CC.OO. are the two major union confederations. CEOE is the predominant employer association, which also has a confederal structure.
Source: (1) *Boletín de Estadísticas Laborales*, various issues; (2) cost-of-living index.

framework regulating the labour market and have affected incomes policies), it is the setting of wage ranges that makes them relevant for collective bargaining and micro-economic flexibility. Given the high coverage of the signing parties and the setting of a usually narrow range of wage increases to be applied economy-wide, these agreements did not allow for adjustment of wages to firm-specific shocks. Some economists claim that this constituted a negative aspect of these agreements. We have already commented that these negative effects, if any, cannot be attributed to the agreements since the sectoral dispersion of wage-rate increases has been low even when the agreements were not in effect. Jimeno and Meixide (1991) confirm, after analysing all the collective agreements registered since 1985, that the existence of an economy-wide agreement did not affect the dispersion of wage-rate increases across bargaining units.

Empirical evidence on wage rigidity and some estimations of the equilibrium rate of unemployment

On the basis of the evolution of wages described above, it is often argued that wage rigidity is very high in the Spanish labour market (and much higher than in other Western European countries), despite the role played by income policies, already described. In this section, we discuss some estimates of wage rigidity to assess to what extent this argument is correct.

Several ways of measuring wage rigidity have been proposed. First, if real wages were perfectly flexible, they would always be equal to the marginal productivity of labour at the full employment level. This observation justifies measures of real wage rigidity based on the difference between real wages and the value of the marginal productivity of labour at the full employment level, that is, the wage gap. The need to estimate this value makes construction of the "wage gap" measure troublesome. In any case, Viñals (1983) is among those who have attempted to measure the Spanish "wage gap". Under some assumptions (a Cobb-Douglas aggregate production function with constant returns to scale) he found an increasing wage gap between 1974 and 1981, when real wages were between 4 and 11 per cent higher that the marginal productivity of labour at the 1974 employment level. This gap is smaller than those calculated for other OECD countries (see the figures presented by De Neubourg, 1989). This implies that, assuming all the OECD countries were affected by the same supply and demand shocks (and there are reasons to believe that these shocks had a greater impact on the Spanish economy), Spanish real wages are "relatively flexible". These results must be treated with caution since, as is well-known, information on labour share of GDP and wage gaps, without precise knowledge of the aggregate production function and the evolution of labour productivity, can be misleading.

Another indicator of real wage flexibility is the ratio between the elasticities of nominal wages with respect to the rate of inflation and unemployment. This indicator measures the increase in unemployment needed to keep inflation constant — because of wage inertia — after a change in the equilibrium real wage. The smaller the response of nominal wages to inflation, and

Table 23.   Nominal and real wage rigidity in OECD countries

	Real wage rigidity $(a_i + \beta_i)^{-1}$	Nominal wage rigidity $(a_2 + \beta_2)(a_i + \beta_i)^{-1}$
Belgium	0.25	0.04
Denmark	0.58	0.08
France	0.23	0.20
Germany (Fed. Rep.)	0.63	0.49
Ireland	0.27	0.31
Italy	0.06	0.14
Netherlands	0.25	0.24
Spain	0.52	0.56
United Kingdom	0.77	0.70
Australia	1.10	0.10
New Zealand	0.23	0.22
Canada	0.32	1.37
United States	0.25	0.80
Japan	0.06	0.05
Austria	0.11	0.46
Finland	0.29	1.01
Norway	0.08	0.37
Sweden	0.08	0.39
Switzerland	0.13	0.41

Source: Layard, Nickell and Jackman (1991), Chapter 9, p. 407.

the larger the response of nominal wages to unemployment, then the more flexible real wages will be and the smaller will be the ratio described above. Obviously, the more flexible real wages are, the smaller and less persistent the wage gap.

This indicator of wage rigidity can be computed after the corresponding Philips curve and wage regressions have been estimated. Dolado and Malo de Molina (1985) have attempted such estimations for Spain and found degrees of wage rigidity which are among the highest in OECD countries (between 2 and 5 in the short run and between 4 and 9 in the long run). This would seem to contradict the results obtained for the wage gap. Another study (Grubb et al., 1983) finds a value of 1.45 for this indicator, which is also among the highest they find for other OECD countries.

Finally, the indicators of real and nominal wage rigidities presented earlier in this chapter, in the section on wage flexibility, can be computed after estimation of the corresponding parameters. A collection of such estimates for several European countries is presented in Layard, Nickell and Jackman (1991, Chapter 9) and reproduced in table 23.

These estimates support the view that wage rigidity in Spain is not particularly high and cannot account for the employment crisis of 1975-85. The study by Layard, Nickell and Jackman aims to explain unemployment across OECD countries using these measures of wage rigidity and other explanatory variables (such as unemployment benefits, percentage of long-term unemployment, mismatch indices). It is not surprising that, in their regressions, Spain appears as an "outlier", and the introduction of a dummy variable is needed to explain Spanish unemployment. The authors' interpretation of this is that the variable corresponds to the wage push of the late 1970s. We believe, however, for the reasons explained in Chapter 1, that it should be interpreted as the effects of the structural change undergone by the Spanish economy at that time.

We end on a note of caution. The studies cited above are subject to the low quality of available statistics on Spanish wages. There are several reasons why the Spanish earnings survey, the data source for most of these studies, overestimates wage increases. In any case, this review leads us to conclude that the empirical evidence is rather mixed and that there are insufficient reasons to believe that the real wage rigidity of the Spanish labour market is not among the highest in Western Europe.

Collective bargaining: The legal framework[8]

As observed earlier, the characteristics of the wage-setting process are, together with the behaviour of unemployed, the most relevant factors for the evolution of wages and unemployment. In Spain, as in most Western European countries, the main form of wage setting is collective bargaining. Hence, it is necessary to review the Spanish collective bargaining system and the legal framework regulating it, to assess to what extent wage rigidities and high equilibrium unemployment are due to them.

In general, there are two types of regulation which may affect collective bargaining and so employers' and workers' "flexibility" to set wages, when collective bargaining is the main wage determination process. The first type of regulation can be referred to as "rules of the game", that is, those legal provisions stating how collective bargaining is to be conducted. The second type of regulation relates to legal provisions constraining the outcomes of collective bargaining. Minimum wage laws and working hours regulations are particularly relevant to labour cost flexibility. However, this second type of regulation is not always universally effective, as employers may find ways of bypassing them when workers' bargaining rights are not sufficiently protected.

"Rules of the game"

In Spain, the "rules of the game" of collective bargaining are basically as follows:

(i)   Collective bargaining is a worker's right recognized by the Workers' Statute (*Ley del Estatuto de los Trabajadores*, LET), the main law regulating the labour market. To exercise it, all workers elect representatives. Elections are held every four years and all workers (not only union members) are eligible. These representatives conduct collective bargaining with employers. In practice, more than 70 per

Table 24. **Number of collective agreements, Spain, 1980-91**

	Total	Enterprise agreements	Industry agreements [1]
1980 [2]	2 564	n.a.	n.a.
1981 [3]	2 694	1 778	916 (34.00)
1982 [4]	3 385	2 186	1 199 (35.42)
1983	3 655	2 376	1 279 (34.99)
1984	3 796	2 539	1 257 (33.11)
1985	3 834	2 590	1 244 (32.45)
1986	3 790	2 588	1 202 (31.72)
1987	4 112	2 817	1 295 (31.49)
1988	4 096	2 826	1 270 (31.01)
1989	4 302	3 016	1 286 (29.89)
1990	4 595	3 254	1 341 (29.18)
1991 [4]	4 668	3 334	1 334 (28.58)

Notes: [1] Percentage (column 3 over column 1) in parenthesis. [2] Excludes agreements in País Vasco [Basque Country] and Cataluña [Catalonia]. [3] Excludes agreements in Cataluña [Catalonia]. [4] Provisional.
Source: *Boletín de Estadísticas Laborales*, July 1991.

cent of the representatives belong to the two major trade union confederations, the UGT (socialist) and the CC.OO. (communist).

(ii) Collective bargaining agreements are legally enforceable and apply to all workers whether or not they are unionized (contrary to what happens in "closed-shop" systems). No worker can be excluded from collective bargaining provisions.

(iii) The structure of collective bargaining is decided between unions and workers' associations on the one hand and employer associations on the other. In practice, collective bargaining takes place at three levels: economy-wide, though agreement is not reached every year, industry and firm (see table 24). Collective agreements reached at industry level are supposed to be binding for all workers and employers in the industry. Only about 75 per cent of wage-earners in the private sector are covered by collective bargaining agreements. Of those, only 15 per cent of workers are covered by collective bargaining agreements reached at the enterprise level. In practice, the effectiveness of collective bargaining agreements reached at the industry level is doubtful. Many workers are employed in small firms, without union protection and without enough information on the provisions of these agreements to ensure that employers comply with them. In addition, their contents are limited mainly to the setting of wages and working hours. As a result, neither the scope nor the depth of collective bargaining is particularly impressive. Table 25 presents some data on the coverage of collective bargaining. These data are produced by the Spanish Ministry of Employment from the register of collective agreements, and do not allow precise calculation of the coverage rate

Table 25.   *Industrial distribution of collective agreements, Spain, 1983 and 1990 (by NACE industries, 1-digit level)*

	1983				1990 [1]			
	Enterprise agreements		Industry agreements		Enterprise agreements		Industry agreements	
	Number	Workers affected	Number	Workers affected	Number	Workers affected	Number	Workers affected
0	22	5 851	43	467 905	32	2 013	43	646 139
1	121	78 868	16	6 111	151	79 514	18	12 296
2	327	128 234	85	347 413	313	100 673	80	308 066
3	448	290 510	65	676 204	500	243 223	65	845 476
4	431	123 865	313	1 120 101	568	124 788	300	1 115 703
5	19	5 057	48	512 725	19	9 139	55	753 432
6	323	54 083	365	1 171 535	408	76 472	382	1 292 194
7	218	226 979	131	204 283	286	207 989	136	199 278
8	56	23 271	41	195 059	127	31 097	50	432 070
9	411	137 912	172	450 311	745	224 766	180	722 185
Total	2 376	1 074 630	1 279	5 151 647	3 149	1 099 674	1 309	6 326 839

[1] Provisional.

Description of Sectors: 0 = Agriculture, 1 = Energy and water distribution, 2 = Mining and chemicals, 3 = Metal industries, 4 = Non-durable manufacturing, 5 = Construction, 6 = Trade, 7 = Transport and communications, 8 = Finance, banking and services to firms, 9 = Social and personal services.

Source: Computed by aggregation of the corresponding data in *Boletín de Estadísticas Laborales*, July 1991.

of collective bargaining. For instance, the number of workers affected by the extension of existing collective agreements is not included in these statistics, and the number of workers affected by collective agreements at the industry level is a subjective estimate by the corresponding bargaining unit.[9] In any event, from these figures we observe that most workers are affected by collective agreements at the industry level (about 70 per cent of wage-earners) while only about 12 per cent of all wage-earners are covered by collective agreements at the enterprise level.[10] The characteristics of collective agreements at industry level regarding their contents and degree of application, to which we shall return later, justify our previous assertion about the scope and depth of collective bargaining in Spain.

(iv) Employers' associations and trade unions or workers' associations can also freely establish rules to govern conflict between collective bargaining agreements. In principle, a collective bargaining agreement in operation cannot be modified by another agreement. In practice, there are few conflicts because the contents of economy-wide agreements are only binding for the parties signing them, and the contents of agreements at industry level are accepted as minimum standards for negotiation at the enterprise level.

(v) There are some conditions under which the Government can extend the scope of application of collective bargaining agreements. When a firm or industrial sector has no collective bargaining agreement in operation, and there are no higher-level agreements which apply, the collective bargaining agreement of a firm or industrial sector in similar economic circumstances may be extended to it. This extension procedure must be initiated by a petition of the employer or the representatives of the workers affected. In practice, the procedure is complicated, which might explain why the number of collective agreements extended since 1985 has averaged only about 14-15 a year.

Because the scope and depth of collective bargaining in Spain are limited, the most important influence on the contents of most employment arrangements are the legal regulations constraining the outcomes of collective bargaining agreements. We describe below the minimum wage laws and working hours limitations, which are relevant for wage flexibility.

Minimum wage laws

The current minimum wage policy, introduced in 1963, consists of a statutory minimum fixed annually by the Government after consultation with trade unions and employer associations. An important feature is discrimination between workers aged under 18 and those aged 18 and over. Unions oppose this discrimination, but the Government justifies it as necessary and similar to practice in other EC countries.

This statutory minimum is binding across the economy without distinction by occupation, work status or contractual relationship with the employer (for instance, temporary or permanent workers). According to the Workers' Statute (LET) the Government must take into account the following when fixing the minimum wage:

(i) cost-of-living index;

(ii) productivity changes;

(iii) the share of workers' compensation in national income; and

(iv) the current economic situation.

In practice, expected inflation is the most important determining factor. There is no pre-established formula on how these variables affect the minimum wage, so the Government enjoys a great deal of discretion.

In addition, the law calls for a review of the statutory minimum wage every six months and when the Government's forecast of inflation is substantially different to actual inflation. In practice, no revision has been proposed in recent years, even though the minimum wage has fallen in real terms.

There are no reliable data on the coverage of the minimum wage. Some estimates suggest that it affects between 2 and 6 per cent of all wage-earners. Indirectly, the minimum wage also affects the income of those receiving unemployment benefits, workers not covered by collective bargaining (about 25 per cent of wage and salary workers) and self-employed workers, whose minimum social security contributions are fixed in relation to the minimum wage. There are no special groups of workers excluded from application of the minimum wage.

Working hours restrictions

Working hours are usually fixed by collective bargaining agreements at the industry and enterprise levels, but there are also some legal restrictions. The maximum number of normal working hours per week is set, by law, at 40 hours. The remuneration of overtime hours is usually included in collective bargaining agreements. The law says that there should be an overtime premium of at least 75 per cent over ordinary hours. The maximum number of overtime hours is restricted to 80 per year per worker. Similarly, night-work hours are remunerated with a premium of at least 25 per cent. Holidays must be at least 12 days per year and paid leave no less than 30 days. The law also stipulates that daily working hours cannot exceed 9 and between full work spells there should be a minimum gap of 12 hours.

Apart from rules on the maximum length of working hours and the premiums the law requires for payment for overtime and night work, there is considerable flexibility in the organization of working hours. The bargaining parties make use of this flexibility and the issue is a common feature of collective bargaining agreements. In recent years, the number of hours agreed in collective bargaining has declined, and this number is usually lower in collective bargaining agreements at the enterprise level.

The characteristics of collective bargaining and wage flexibility

The "rules of the game" described above and the minimum wage and working hours regulations do not impose a great burden on wage setters. Thus, it can be concluded that the wage determination process is rather "flexible" or, more precisely, employers and workers enjoy a great deal of discretion when setting wages and other employment conditions; and that the degrees of real and nominal rigidity in the wage-setting process reflect the objectives of the bargaining parties. In other words, workers' and employers' behaviour is the main determinant of wage rigidities. We now turn to a discussion of the main characteristics of the collective bargaining process which result from this "flexibility" and their economic consequences.

Among these characteristics, the degree of centralization of collective bargaining, the duration of collective bargaining agreements and the degree of indexation of nominal wage rates are the most important factors affecting wage rigidity. The degree of centralization of collective bargaining is a key determinant of the equilibrium unemployment rate and of real and nominal wage flexibility, since it affects the response of wages to the unemployment rate (the value of the parameter α_1 in wage equation [1] on p. 60). The more centralized the wage-setting process, the higher this parameter and so the lower the equilibrium unemployment rate and real and nominal wage rigidity. There are several reasons for this: first, national wage setters internalize the macroeconomic effects of wage increases and, therefore, are more responsive to unemployment (α_1 is higher); second, at the national level the alternative wage for union members is lower, since by definition there are no other sectors of the economy offering alternative employment as there are in the case of decentralized bargaining; third, "insider effects" are absent; fourth,

Table 26.   Number of collective agreements registered each month, Spain, average 1985-90

January	411.8
February	335.2
March	260.5
April	315.8
May	398.3
June	432.2
July	478.5
August	499.8
September	245.5
October	326.5
November	218.8
December	148.8
Total	4 071.7

Source: Computed from data provided by the Ministry of Employment.

the elasticity of the labour demand curve, which determines the wage resulting from bargaining, is generally higher at the national level; and, finally, as stressed by Blanchard and Summers (1988), there are "fiscal increasing returns" which can be used as incentives for wage moderation.[11] Additionally, when there are unanticipated shocks to labour productivity, the differences between actual unemployment and equilibrium unemployment are smaller the higher the degree of centralization of the wage-setting process, as showed by Jimeno (1991b). On the other hand, the shorter the duration of collective bargaining agreements or the larger the number of agreements specifying cost-of-living allowances, the greater the nominal wage flexibility. Similarly, the larger the degree of synchronization of agreements, the smaller nominal wage flexibility.

We have already commented that the degree of centralization of collective bargaining depends on several factors and does not depend, exclusively, on the level at which collective bargaining is carried out. Furthermore, it depends on the coordination among bargaining units and the synchronization of collective agreements. Whenever bargaining units are established at the national (economy-wide) level, coordination among them is high and/or there is high degree of time synchronization, hence credible national wage guidelines can be put in place that affect bargaining at different levels. A negative aspect of economy-wide bargaining is the limited degree of micro-economic flexibility implied by this type of collective bargaining, to the extent that the outcomes are imposed on bargaining units at lower levels of negotiation. However, where there is scope for "wage drift", defined as the difference between wage-rate increases at the economy-wide level and actual wage-rate increases at the firm level, micro-economic flexibility arises.[12]

In Spain, collective bargaining takes place throughout the year, that is, the degree of synchronization is low (see table 26). Additionally, as table 24 shows, there is an excessive number of bargaining units (and coordination among them is not always high). It is true that about 80-85 per cent of workers' representatives for collective bargaining belong to the two main trade union confederations (UGT and CC.OO.) and that these confederations have a structure that is effective in achieving internal coordination. However, coordination between them seems problematic, especially in election years, and coordination among employers almost non-existent. Additionally, as we saw earlier, there have been no economy-wide wage agreements, which could have established credible wage guidelines, and hence coordination, since 1986. Therefore, it is not surprising that the general view of the wage-setting process in Spain is that it is somewhat decentralized, raising equilibrium unemployment and the difference between actual unemployment and equilibrium unemployment during disinflationary periods or after negative supply shocks.

For the reasons sketched above, this decentralization of collective bargaining has had negative macroeconomic implications, both in terms of unemployment and inflation (see Jimeno, 1992). On the other hand, it has not achieved micro-economic flexibility, as the dispersion of wage growth across industrial sectors has been minimal. During the 1978-86 period, the blame for this lack of flexibility was put on the national agreements which serve as instruments of incomes policies, because of the excessively narrow wage range established by these agreements. However, after 1986, when no such agreement has been in effect, micro-economic flexibility has not been significantly higher (see the data on wage growth dispersion in table 20). The cause for this is the "egalitarian" strategy in collective bargaining (that is, they have set similar wage-rate increase targets in all units, both at firm and sectoral level, without consideration of the economic conditions of each unit) that unions have successfully pursued.[13]

On the other hand, there does not seem to be a significant wage drift (the difference between workers' earnings growth and wage rate growth). Although there are few studies on the magnitude of wage drift in Spain or its sectoral dispersion, mainly because of the low quality of the data available on the evolution of workers' earnings, the evolution of wage drift is almost exclusively related to labour composition effects (changes in the characteristics of employed workers) rather than economic circumstances of firms or industries. Concretely, Albarracín and Artola (1990) show that, for reasons related to the increasing turnover rate associated with the increase in fixed-term employment, the wage drift has even been negative in some years. Jimeno and Meixide (1991) confirm this finding by analysing the sectoral dispersion of the wage drift and fixed-term employment.

The existence of cost-of-living allowances or productivity clauses in collective agreements and their duration are also key determinants of nominal wage rigidity, since they affect how "inflation surprises" are translated into real wages (i.e., the parameter α_2 in the wage equation [1] on p. 60). Table 27 presents some information on the duration of collective bargaining agreements. It shows that roughly half of collective bargaining agreements are for one year; among those with a longer duration, most are revised during the period in which they are in effect. Table 28 shows that relatively few collective bargaining agreements contain clauses on productivity (about 25 per cent). The percentage of workers affected by collective bargaining agreements with clauses on productivity is similar. In addition, about 55 per cent of workers covered by collective bargaining agreements are entitled to cost-of-living allowances. However, economy-wide agreements,

Table 27. Duration of collective agreements, Spain, 1988 and 1989

	1988		1989 [1]	
	Number of agreements	Number of workers (000)	Number of agreements	Number of workers (000)
Total	4 096	6 864.7	4 131	6 672.8
More than 1 year	1 035	1 866.9	1 158	1 984.5
1 year	2 065	2 382.9	2 147	2 561.8
Revisions	996	2 614.9	826	2 126.5
Industry level	1 270	5 794.3	1 233	5 647.4
More than 1 year	262	1 602.6	302	1 565.8
1 year	682	2 102.0	710	2 239.8
Revisions	326	2 089.7	221	1 841.7
Enterprise level	2 826	1 070.4	2 898	1 025.5
More than 1 year	773	264.3	856	418.6
1 year	1 383	280.9	1 437	322.0
Revisions	670	525.2	605	284.8

[1] Provisional.
Source: Ministerio de Trabajo y Seguridad Social: *Estadísticas de convenios colectivos, 1988-89.*

Table 28. Collective bargaining agreements containing special clauses, Spain, 1988

	All agreements		Industry level		Enterprise level	
	Number	Number of workers (000)	Number	Number of workers (000)	Number	Number of workers (000)
Productivity	945	2 059.2	178	1 616.1	767	443.1
Absenteeism	618	1 497.4	95	1 216.3	523	281.1
Labour Relations	2 414	4 818.1	701	3 990.4	1 713	827.7
COLA [1]	1 221	3 753.1	476	3 285.4	745	467.7

[1] Cost-of-living allowances.
Source: Ministerio de Trabajo y Seguridad Social: *Anuario de Estadísticas Laborales,* 1990.

when in effect, have often stipulated revision of wage-rate increases contingent on the behaviour of inflation.

The impression one gets from these figures is that the degree of indexation of nominal wages rates within the year is rather low, although the relatively short duration of agreements and the frequency of revisions suggest that nominal flexibility increases after a year.[14]

In any case and as a main conclusion to this section, it should be stressed that all these characteristics of the collective bargaining process result from the free interaction of employers' and workers' representatives and are not conditioned by "excessive" legal regulation. In this sense, then, we conclude that the wage determination process in Spain is "rather flexible", even though the indices of real and nominal wage rigidity defined above may be high.

Concluding remarks

In this chapter we have reviewed the behaviour of wages, the concept of the equilibrium unemployment rate and the influence of labour market institutions from the perspective of the Spanish experience. We have concluded that collective bargaining, the main process determining wages in Spain, is a rather "flexible" system, in the sense that the bargaining units have a great deal of discretion when setting wages. However, there are some characteristics of the process, mainly the degree of decentralization, which negatively affect the equilibrium unemployment rate and the unemployment-inflation trade-off without contributing to micro-economic flexibility. In the end, the degree of nominal and real wage flexibility depends on the behaviour of wage setters. The available empirical evidence on this issue is mixed, and the low quality of the data makes it difficult to reach definite conclusions. It seems, however, that there has been an increase in the equilibrium unemployment rate, and this needs to be considered carefully. Policies to reverse this trend should concentrate on the structure of collective bargaining, the unemployment protection system and employment policies to improve training and the efficiency of public employment agencies.

The future prospects of wage determination in Spain are obviously linked to the creation of the EC's single market, the European Monetary Union (EMU) and the institution of a common social policy. All this development will affect the functioning and, possibly, the legal regulation of the labour markets of member countries.

The single European market affects wage determination because, in general, a higher degree of competition on product markets translates into more elastic labour demand curves and less scope for unwarranted wage increases. Once unit labour costs converge across member countries and devaluation of the currency is not a policy option, the wage determination process in each member country is constrained by the evolution of wages and productivity in the others. The question is then to what extent this convergence in unit labour costs has already been achieved. According to European Community data (mentioned in the 1991 *Employment Report*), unit labour costs are very similar across member countries at this stage. Thus, in a single market with similar labour unit costs across member countries, significant restrictions for wage setting arise, and it is important that wage setters recognize these restrictions.

Two issues arise from this. The first, the subject of current debate, refers to the desirability of a coordinated wage determination process across member countries (collective bargaining at the "European" level). Our previous comments on the effects of centralization of the wage determination process apply here. We believe that coordination must be achieved either explicitly, by creating the necessary institutions, or implicitly, by means of a credible European monetary policy. At the same time, there must be scope for (micro-economic) wage flexibility, so that wages can support the adjustment of sectors and firms in special situations. In any case, as the use of monetary and fiscal policies is increasingly constrained, income policies will have to play a greater role in regional stabilization programmes. Second, in the Spanish case, one may question whether changes already taking place in the wage determination process are sufficient to meet those restrictions. As previously noted, the trade union confederations (UGT and CC.OO.) have pursued an "egalitarian" strategy in the sense of proposing similar wage-rate increases across all sectors and firms in the economy. This strategy has been successful, as indicated by the low dispersion of wage-rate increases, even since 1986, when no economy-wide agreement has been in effect. The two confederations have recently indicated a change of policy regarding collective bargaining after 1991,[15] according to which labour productivity will replace expected inflation as the main determinant of wage-rate increases. But the main drawbacks of the Spanish wage-setting system arise from the structure and the low scope and depth of collective bargaining issues which are not sufficiently addressed.

Notes

[1] See Blanchard and Kiyotaki (1987).

[2] For simplicity, we have not included "hysteresis effects" in wage and price determination. "Hysteresis effects" arise when not only current unemployment but also past unemployment affect wage and price determination.

[3] Additionally, when hysteresis effects are present we need to distinguish between equilibrium rates of unemployment in the short run and in the long run, the latter being a linear combination of the short-run equilibrium unemployment rate and past unemployment (see below).

[4] Note that equations [1] and [2] reduce to $u = [\alpha_0 + \beta_0 + z - (\alpha_2 + \beta_2)(dp - dp^e)](\alpha_1 + \beta_1)^{-1}]$.

[5] It is conceivable that this might have happened during the late 1970s in Spain, when political reforms raised expectations of higher living standards among workers. However, the policy of wage restraint adopted by trade unions during the early 1980s suggests that the realization of these expectations was deferred.

[6] See Lindbeck and Snower (1988) and Layard and Bean (1990) for the plausible different role of "insiders" and "outsiders" in wage determination.

[7] There is some debate about the existence of a "hump-shaped" relationship. We shall return to this issue below.

[8] A more detailed description of collective bargaining practices in Spain can be found in Jimeno and Toharia (1991a), on which this section draws.

[9] For more on this point, see Jimeno (1991a), Chapter 7.

[10] See Jimeno and Meixide (1991) for the evolution of the coverage rate of collective bargaining by industry and type of agreement.

[11] For some studies on the relationship between centralization of the wage-setting process and economic performance, see Bruno and Sachs (1986), Calmfors and Driffill (1988), and Freeman (1988).

[12] This does not imply that a centralized wage-setting process with "wage drift" is equivalent to decentralized wage setting (see Jimeno, 1991b).

[13] In November 1991, the two trade union confederations announced that the "egalitarian" strategy is to be abandoned and agreements will be reached in accordance with the economic circumstances of each bargaining unit. We will comment further on this announcement in the final section of this chapter.

[14] Jimeno (1992) finds that wages rate growth are not affected by "inflation surprises".

[15] See *El País*, 9 Nov. 1991.

Chapter 4

Employment flexibility

> *... Our more recent experience shows that structural reform should pursue greater flexibilization of our labour market. To confirm this, it is enough to recall that a labour market as rigid as the one existing from 1957 until 1977 was unable to exploit a long period of strong economic growth to create employment on a large scale. Between 1957 and 1977 barely 875,000 net jobs were created ... In contrast with these results, the labour market flexibilization initiated in the mid-1980s was clearly superior as a development strategy, both in terms of efficiency and in terms of equity. Between 1985 and 1991, the possibilities created by the reform of employment contracts allowed the economic boom to be exploited, making this period the one with the highest employment growth ever. Between 1985 and 1991, 1,750,000 net jobs were created, that is, in five years of flexible labour market twice as much employment was created as in the 20 years of the Spanish "economic miracle".*
>
> (Translation from *Programa de Convergencia [Spanish Government's Convergence Programme]*, pp. 30-31)

Introduction

As defined in Chapter 3, employment flexibility is equivalent to the absence of legal constraints on firms in their choices at the level of their workforce. Thus, the most important factor determining the degree of employment flexibility is the existence of hiring and firing regulations. In the Spanish case, as in most Western European countries, hiring regulations do not impose a heavy burden, since most take the form of employment programmes designed to encourage the hiring of disadvantaged workers.[1] More important in this respect is the legal ban on private employment agencies and the ineffectiveness of the existing public employment offices (an issue to which we return in Chapter 5).

However, it has been argued that Spanish firing regulations are too restrictive and that they impose substantial firing costs.[2] In fact, the whole debate on labour market flexibility in Spain has been centred on this issue.[3] Probably as a consequence, the main policy advocated and then adopted as a response to the unemployment problem has been the liberalization of fixed-term employment. Many economists and policy-makers argue that this reform has been decisive in the post-1985 employment recovery (see, for instance, the quotation at the beginning of this chapter), a view we do not share. While the 1984 legal changes had *some* positive effect on employment creation, although not as large as is often argued, they had also unintended consequences on productivity, wages, labour turnover, unemployment duration and, hence, on public finances through the evolution of expenses relating to unemployment subsidies, and on the "precariousness" of employment.

In this chapter, we first review the Spanish (employment) flexibility debate, arguing that employment rigidity was not as high in Spain as was claimed by those blaming it as a major contributor to the employment crisis of 1975-85. We then describe the legal reform of employment contracts introduced in late 1984 to assess their effects on the functioning of the labour market. We do this in four stages: description of the regulations on labour contracts and firings; analysis of the incidence of fixed-term employment; consideration of the influence of fixed-term employment on job creation during the post-1985 recovery period and other consequences of fixed-term employment. We conclude with some comments on the current employment flexibility of the Spanish labour market.

The "rigidity" of the Francoist labour market and the employment crisis (1975-85)

One of the best and most influential books on the Spanish labour market (Serrano and Malo de Molina, 1978) argued that the Francoist labour market was based on the combination of a very flexible wage-setting process coupled with a very rigid employment system which *de facto* guaranteed lifetime jobs to workers in exchange for compliance on wages and political acquiescence. In fact, the Francoist system did allow dismissals for workforce adjustment (those related to union or political activities were considered disciplinary dismissals and hence carried no costs for the employer). However, dismissals for economic reasons were considered "unwarranted" and hence usually involved severance payments, the level of which was left to the discretion of the judge deciding the case. Additionally, in the case of collective dismissals (the so-called *expedientes de regulación de empleo*, hereafter referred to as ERE), an administrative procedure had to be followed. However, this did not mean that ERE were denied; denial was the exception rather than the rule.

In addition, the system did not mean that all labour contracts were indefinite in nature. Temporary contracts, i.e. contracts whose duration lasted as long as the job (a very common contractual form in such strongly seasonal activities as agriculture and construction, and also used in other sectors such as tourism), were legal and widely used. The scant evidence available on that matter suggests that in the late 1960s, as many as 20 per cent of all employees in some sectors (those cited above) had a temporary contract. It is true, however, that this percentage tended to decline over time as a consequence of actions undertaken by the still-illegal unions.

On Franco's death in 1975, the emergent trade unions pursued major campaigns to restore purchasing power and to limit the employers' ability to adjust their workforces at will. In a demagogic move to maintain Francoism without Franco, the first government of the restored monarchy passed a labour relations law which required the reinstatement of unfairly dismissed workers without the possibility of severance payments as a substitute. Although the section of the law containing this provision was repealed six months after its passage, it illustrates how troubled the immediate aftermath of the death of the dictator was (in particular in 1976, until the Political Reform Act was passed at the end of that year, paving the way for a clearly democratic regime).

The regulation of strikes and the legalization of trade unions in early 1977 led to the negotiation of the Moncloa Pacts (already discussed in Chapter 3). These contained a number of agreements not only on wage restraint but also on the possibility of introducing fixed-term contracts as well as training and apprenticeship contracts for youngsters. Over the following two years, after the approval of the new Constitution in 1978, intense negotiations between unions, employers and the Government permitted the final passage in early 1980 of the *Ley del Estatuto de los Trabajadores* [the Workers' Statute] (LET), which was to become the cornerstone of Spanish labour law.

Despite this new law, many commentators still claimed that the Spanish labour market was too rigid. The argument had two strands. On the one hand, it was claimed that firing costs imposed excessive burdens on enterprises. On the other hand, Spain was cited as the OECD country with the highest average seniority of workers in their firms, a fact attributed to very low labour mobility. Both of these claims were disputed by Toharia (1985b). He argued that the very fact that the number of redundancies had been so high in the 1980-85 period (with 2 million people fired for economic or technological reasons) was *prima facie* evidence that they were not *too* costly. Severance payments were on average relatively modest. Finally, collective redundancies were approved in more than 90 per cent of cases. On the second claim, regarding seniority, the evidence on high average seniority came from a survey of large firms and was not representative of the economy as a whole. When new evidence became available, it was shown that the percentage of "senior" workers (those with at least five years' seniority) was somewhat higher than elsewhere in Europe, but much lower than had been suggested. This higher percentage could be considered normal in an economy such as Spain's, which had suffered tremendous labour shedding during the 1975-85 employment crisis (see Chapter 1). Contrary to the claim that mobility was low, Toharia computed estimates of "natural wastage" (i.e. the number of separations which imply no cost for the firms) in the Spanish economy, showing that these were far from negligible.

In general, it is difficult to blame the employment crisis of 1975 to 1985 on the lack of employment flexibility of the Spanish economy. Firms could dismiss workers, especially after 1980, more or less automatically, even though this was not without costs. However, had these costs not existed, the redundancies would have been resisted by the trade unions, and this would have aggravated even further the economic situation of firms and would have led to further employment losses. On the other hand, although mobility was low, as could be expected in an economy suffering strong employment declines, it was not nil.

The regulation of employment contracts and firings

In this section we describe the legal framework affecting employment contracts that arose from the approval of the Workers' Statute (LET) in 1980 and its reform in late 1984. These two legal developments modified and clarified a number of aspects which had become ineffective during the years of breakdown of the old regime and during the political transition to democracy. The main influence of the LET on these regulations was to widen the grounds for economic and technological redundancies and to impose stricter limits on the discretion previously enjoyed by judges in settling dismissal cases. It also established well-defined periods for the resolution of collective dismissals (establishing a maximum length of two months for their approval).

As already mentioned, the "typical" employment contract establishes a permanent and full-time relationship between employer and employee. Currently, the regulations affecting the dismissal of workers employed under this contract are similar to those in other Western European countries (see Emerson, 1988). These regulations distinguish between individual dismissals and collective dismissals, on the one hand, and between dismissals for economic reasons (redundancies) and firings for disciplinary reasons, on the other. In general, employers can dismiss any worker after at least 30 days' notice, with a severance payment related to the worker's seniority. Severance payments for "fair" dismissals are fixed at 20 days' wages per year of seniority (with a maximum of 12 months' wages). Dismissed workers may sue employers in the labour courts. There is compulsory conciliation and, in case of failure, the case is settled by a judge. If the settlement favours the worker, that is, if the judge declares the dismissal "unfair" (or "unwarranted"), severance payments are increased up to 45 days' wages per year of seniority (with a maximum of 42 months' wages). In the case of disciplinary firings, the judge may also order the reinstatement of the worker although, in practice, this rarely happens. On the other hand, collective dismissals (ERE) must be approved in advance by the Government's labour inspectorate. In this case, severance payments are similar to those for the case of (individual) "fair dismissals". Usually, these ERE are negotiated between employers' and workers' representatives and, in case of agreement, administrative approval is automatic. One aspect of these negotiations is the amount of the severance payments, which ends up being higher than that established by the law. In the case of disagreement, administrative approval is less likely but still possible and, if granted, it is also usual that the severance payments are raised to those corresponding to (individual) "unfair" dismissals. In fact, even in the case of disagreement between workers' representatives and employers, administrative approval is almost always granted, although severance payments might be raised to those corresponding to "unfair" dismissal. This administrative intervention on collective dismissals is still criticized from time to time by employers who complain about the restriction on their freedom to dismiss workers as they see fit. There are reasons to believe, however, that this is to be seen more as a political gesture to be revived as convenient than a real complaint.

These regulations are not very restrictive when compared to other Western European countries (see Emerson, 1988). Only the amount of severance payments in the case of "unfair" dismissals is larger than in most of these countries. Thus, the issue is whether the scope for "warranted" dismissal is wide enough. In any case, in practice, most firings are settled in the preliminary conciliatory hearing, which adds some degree of automaticity to the process (Fernández, Muro and Toharia, 1988). Even for collective dismissals, workers' representatives and employers often agree beforehand on the number of redundancies and the severance payments to be paid to dismissed workers, as already mentioned.

In addition to the indefinite labour contract, which is considered the "normal" contract, the LET also allows two types of temporary or fixed-term contract, although they were not widely used before 1984. At that time, following the arguments of some employers and economists who blamed the employment crisis on employment rigidity, the Spanish Government introduced new regulations to enlarge the scope of fixed-term employment contracts. Consequently, Spanish employers can now choose among the following employment contracts when hiring a new employee, in addition to the "normal" permanent full-time employment contract:

(i)   Contracts for temporary jobs. These employment contracts do not entail any severance payments in the case of dismissals, nor they are restricted to a fixed tenure.

(ii) Fixed-term contracts. They require a minimum tenure of six months (one year, after April 1992) and can be extended up to a maximum of three years. There are no limits to the percentage of workers in a firm who can be employed under these contracts. In case of dismissal or non-conversion of the contract into a permanent one at the end of the maximum three-year tenure, workers receive a severance payment of 12 days' wages per year of seniority (not 20-45 days' wages, as for dismissed permanent workers). The difference between this type of contract and the temporary contract cited above lies in the nature of the job. For fixed-term contracts, it is not necessary that the job be temporary.

(iii) Training and apprenticeship contracts for youngsters, which are limited in terms of tenure (minimum three months; maximum three years), in terms of age (the employee must be no older than 20 years), and in terms of qualifications (in the case of apprenticeship contracts, the employee must have finished formal education within the previous four years, but the interpretation of "formal education" is, in practice, very lenient). These contracts entail substantial reductions in the social security contributions paid by the employer.

Additionally, two further comments ought to be made. First, part-time contracts are also possible, although in practice they are rarely used, as we shall see below. This is presumably because they impose, on a proportional basis, the same obligations on the employer's side as full-time contracts and because of the importance of the non-wage component of labour costs (see Chapter 5). Secondly, temporary work agencies are not regulated. Although they do exist, they are believed to be illegal. Unfortunately, their importance in the composition of fixed-term employment is unknown.

The main characteristic of fixed-term employment contracts is that they involve substantially lower firing costs than the typical permanent contract. Not only are severance payments lower but, more importantly, there are some provisions protecting dismissed permanent workers which do not apply to workers employed under fixed-term contracts. For instance, after a permanent worker is fired, the worker may sue the employer and obtain significantly higher severance payments, depending on whether the labour court declares the dismissal "fair" or "unfair" (or on the probability thereof, which may influence a likely pre-court agreement). Obviously, the uncertainty of this outcome and the administrative costs involved in the process are important for the employer when considering dismissing a permanent worker. Conversely, workers employed under fixed-term employment contracts cannot sue the employer in case of dismissal. In this sense, dismissals of fixed-term employees are automatic and involve much lower costs. The difference between both pecuniary and non-pecuniary firing costs between workers employed under different labour contracts introduces a rather peculiar two-tier system in employment relations. Although similar arrangements exist in other Western European countries, the high percentage of workers with fixed-term employment contracts in Spain has no parallel. For this reason, the evolution of this type of employment in Spain constitutes an interesting object of analysis to help our understanding of the effects of increasing "labour market flexibility" by promoting fixed-term employment.

The incidence of fixed-term employment

In this section we look at the distribution of employment under fixed-term contracts (see Chapter 1 for a general analysis of the evolution of employment by types of contract). More detailed information on this matter can be found in Segura et al. (1991), this being the main source for the data we use (their data come, in turn, from the *Labour Force Survey*). To analyse the incidence of fixed-term employment, we first present the rates of fixed-term employment by several personal characteristics of those employed under this type of contract. Then we compare permanent workers' and fixed-term workers' characteristics and estimate the probability of becoming a permanent worker after entering employment in the previous year under a fixed-term employment contract.

Thus, table 29 shows the proportion of employment under fixed-term contracts by selected personal characteristics of workers. While women tend to have a higher rate of fixed-term employment, the rate for males more than doubled over the three-year 1987-90 period. Although incidence rates have increased for all groups, fixed-term work is clearly age-related: two in three workers aged 20-24 work under such a contract, a proportion that rises to four our of five for those younger than 20. Data on education and occupation suggest that those with higher qualifications and in more skilled occupations tend to have lower rates of fixed-

Table 29.   Incidence of fixed-term contracts by worker characteristics, Spain, 1987-90

	1987	1988	1989	1990
Total	15.6	22.4	26.6	29.8
Gender				
Males	14.4	20.5	24.5	27.8
Females	18.4	26.8	31.2	34.2
Age groups				
16-19	48.2	65.1	74.0	77.9
20-24	31.6	48.9	55.1	61.7
25-29	18.8	27.5	34.3	39.6
30-34	11.6	16.1	20.4	23.3
35-39	10.0	13.7	15.5	18.8
40-44	9.1	12.2	16.5	17.2
45-49	9.4	12.4	13.8	15.3
50-54	8.0	12.2	12.7	14.3
55-59	7.6	9.5	10.0	12.5
60-64	7.1	7.0	8.3	8.8
65 +	4.9	8.4	9.7	8.4
Level of education				
Illiterate	29.2	36.5	36.5	35.9
No studies	20.6	27.0	29.3	32.9
Primary education	13.8	19.2	23.7	26.7
Low-secondary education	20.4	31.6	36.8	41.0
Upper-secondary education	12.2	17.1	20.0	22.4
Vocational training, 1st level	24.3	37.2	43.2	46.8
Vocational training, 2nd level	16.5	24.8	29.0	32.3
University 1st level diploma	9.0	11.0	14.7	14.9
University 3 years, no diploma	15.8	22.8	23.5	26.3
University graduates	9.4	13.2	13.8	17.3
Industries				
Agriculture	39.4	47.2	49.6	50.6
Energy and water	4.4	7.0	8.1	9.4
Mining and chemicals	8.2	12.7	16.6	20.6
Engineering	7.8	14.0	19.2	21.6
Other manufacturing industry	15.3	23.6	27.4	29.7
Construction	29.5	42.3	49.4	54.1
Trade and hotels	18.3	25.6	31.7	35.8
Transport and communications	7.8	10.8	15.9	18.9
Financial institutions, etc.	8.5	12.4	19.3	25.2
Other services	11.7	17.4	19.4	22.0
Occupational groups				
Professionals & technicians	10.1	13.9	14.8	17.7
Managers	2.5	3.6	4.0	4.7
Administrative workers	9.1	13.6	17.4	20.3
Salespeople	14.3	20.9	26.4	32.3
Other service workers	16.9	25.9	31.3	34.4
Agricultural workers	39.2	46.7	50.2	51.7
Production workers	16.3	24.6	30.3	34.2
Armed forces	1.0	2.0	0.5	1.6

(table concluded overleaf)

Table 29 (cont.)

	1987	1988	1989	1990
Total	15.6	22.4	26.6	29.8
Private/public sector				
Private sector	17.8	25.7	30.8	34.4
Public sector	7.9	10.7	12.0	14.0
Region				
Andalucía	21.5	32.2	33.6	36.8
Aragón	16.6	21.1	27.0	24.9
Asturias	10.3	17.9	23.2	23.9
Baleares	15.5	20.3	26.4	30.3
Canarias	25.2	29.8	31.7	36.7
Cantabria	12.9	12.7	21.0	24.6
Castilla-La Mancha	14.4	26.5	34.3	37.1
Castilla y León	14.6	22.9	28.4	30.2
Cataluña	17.0	22.6	25.9	32.2
Comunidad Valenciana	21.0	27.8	30.3	36.1
Extremadura	26.9	27.2	31.6	37.5
Galicia	9.6	15.9	24.8	26.4
Madrid	5.4	8.6	14.0	15.7
Murcia	27.3	34.4	40.8	44.9
Navarra	13.6	26.2	30.2	27.3
País Vasco	10.1	19.0	25.1	23.8
La Rioja	26.5	24.9	27.6	28.9
Working time arrangements				
Full-time	14.2	21.2	25.4	28.6
Part-time	43.9	48.2	53.3	56.7
Usual weekly working hours				
None	41.8	39.2	59.3	38.3
10 or less	46.2	61.2	59.0	57.1
11 to 25	41.8	45.8	50.6	56.7
26 to 30	18.8	21.7	26.7	26.7
31 to 35	15.7	18.5	21.3	25.0
36 to 40	14.1	21.2	25.6	28.7
41 to 45	14.4	22.4	25.8	31.1
46 or more	15.2	20.5	25.9	29.7
Job search				
Is looking for another job	69.1	74.2	74.1	77.2
Is not looking	13.0	20.8	25.4	28.9
Situation one year before				
Working	9.2	14.5	18.2	21.7
Looking for work	61.0	72.1	77.3	81.5
Available but not looking	51.9	65.4	75.2	75.1
Military service	50.6	71.1	71.1	81.3
Student	51.1	69.5	73.4	81.4
Other situation	35.8	52.2	59.3	59.9

Source: *Labour Force Survey.*

term employment, whereas the industrial breakdown shows that agriculture and construction have by far the highest rates, even though the increase over the period applies to all sectors. Other figures in the table suggest that the increase has occurred in both the private and public sectors, the rates being higher in the former, and in all regions, the differences there reflecting the industry mix.

Two other interesting results in table 29 relate to the higher incidence of fixed-term contracts among part-timers and those looking for another job. In both cases, the rates have increased, but not by much (the levels were already very high at the beginning). One possible explanation may lie in the job seniority of these two groups. Since fixed-term contracts and job seniority are (inversely) related and employment growth has taken place through this type of contract, it follows that part-timers and jobseekers tend to be less senior than other workers and will thus tend to have a higher rate of fixed-term work.

From the reported situation of individuals 12 months before the survey date, we can observe a clear relationship between seniority and fixed-term work: "new employees" have a much higher incidence of fixed-term contracts. These figures show two interesting features. First, for "new employees", achieving permanent contract status does not appear to depend much on the previous situation, with the exception of "others" (people outside the labour force). Second, the percentage of "senior" workers with a fixed-term contract has also increased, suggesting that this type of work is a lasting phenomenon. The probability that workers employed under fixed-term contracts will continue in this situation has increased relative to that of gaining permanent status.

Table 30 compares the characteristics of permanent workers and workers employed under fixed-term contracts. From this table, we observe the following patterns:

(i)   Fixed-term workers are younger than permanent ones, and the differences appear to be increasing over time in the case of males. The mean ages and the distribution indicators suggest, once again, that fixed-term contracts have become the normal entry pattern into employment.

(ii) Permanent workers have a higher level of education than their fixed-term counterparts, which is interesting since in general younger workers are better educated. It must be noticed, however, that most educated workers have a lower fixed-term employment rate (see table 29) so that the fact that permanent workers are, on average, better educated is not contradictory with the fact that new entrants into employment, mostly under fixed-term employment contracts, have a higher education degree.

(iii) The above result is confirmed by the analysis of occupational groups: professional and technical workers have a higher weight in permanent work than in work under fixed-term contracts, and this proportion is increasing. Meanwhile, the proportion of non-agricultural production workers has fallen slightly among those with permanent employment, whereas it has grown rapidly within the ranks of workers with fixed-term contracts.

Table 30. Characteristics of fixed-term and permanent workers, by gender, Spain, 1987 and 1990

	Males				Females			
	1987		1990		1987		1990	
	Permanent	Fixed-term	Permanent	Fixed-term	Permanent	Fixed-term	Permanent	Fixed-term
Total (thousands)	4 793.0	809.4	4 543.3	1 748.7	1 842.7	416.5	1 923.5	1 001.7
Average age	40.1	31.5	41.0	30.4	35.4	28.7	36.8	28.5
% of people aged less than 25	10.8	38.3	7.2	39.2	21.7	50.5	13.7	45.8
% of people aged less than 30	23.0	56.3	18.6	59.4	40.1	67.2	31.1	66.4
Average education level (in years)	7.3	6.6	7.8	7.2	8.4	7.8	9.0	8.4
% with at least secondary-level education	25.8	19.2	32.3	22.8	36.7	29.4	44.2	35.9
% with some university education	11.7	5.2	14.0	4.9	19.5	13.1	23.6	13.1
% in agriculture	6.3	21.3	4.7	10.9	0.9	8.2	1.0	4.5
% in manufacturing	36.3	22.1	35.6	24.6	20.8	21.7	19.0	21.4
% in construction	9.7	24.3	9.4	28.7	0.6	0.8	0.7	1.9
% in services	47.7	32.3	50.3	35.8	77.6	69.3	79.2	72.2
% of professionals/technicians	9.7	5.2	11.7	5.1	20.4	12.7	23.6	12.2
% of production workers	51.1	54.1	49.3	63.3	16.1	23.8	14.4	20.2
Average number of hours actually worked	37.8	36.7	37.1	37.2	34.9	32.0	33.6	32.8
Average number of hours usually worked	41.2	40.0	40.9	40.7	38.1	34.7	37.9	36.0
% of self-declared part-time	0.8	6.3	0.5	2.4	9.4	27.9	7.7	18.1
% of working usually less than 26 hrs./wk.	0.8	5.1	0.5	2.0	8.2	24.1	7.1	17.2
% of working usually more than 40 hrs./wk.	20.7	19.2	13.8	13.7	14.2	15.0	8.5	10.2
% looking for another job	1.2	19.9	0.4	4.2	3.2	22.3	1.2	7.0
% working in the private sector of the economy	77.1	89.3	75.3	91.7	70.3	86.7	65.4	85.4

Source: Labour Force Survey.

(iv) Weekly hours actually worked are slightly lower in the case of workers under fixed-term contracts, but there is a trend towards homogenization. We have also computed two indicators related to the extremes of the distribution of hours worked, to control for the possible existence of a greater proportion of part-timers among workers under fixed-term contracts, together with a higher proportion of "exploited" workers among full-timers. The results indicate that while it is true that part-time working is more prevalent among those with fixed-term contracts, the gap is diminishing. The proportion of people working more than 40 hours per week (our indicator of "exploitation") tends to be slightly higher in the case of permanent workers, even though there appears to be a trend towards equalization. The only exception appears to be women in the private sector in 1989 and 1990, but the differences are in any case minor.

(v) With respect to job search, the proportion of workers under fixed-term contracts looking for another job is greater than for permanent workers. However, the interesting fact is that the proportion has markedly diminished over time.

Finally, one can compare the characteristics of those entering employment over the previous 12 months who received a permanent contract and those who remained on a fixed-term employment contract. To do so, we have fitted a logit model aimed at explaining the probability that "new employees" would have a permanent contract. We chose the second quarter of 1987 and the second quarter of 1990, dates at which the *Labour Force Survey* offers information about workers' situation one year before. Hence, we take all employed workers who were not employed one year before (dropping those also declaring a seniority of more than one year, because of inconsistency). Our sample size is 4,836 workers for 1987 and 6,256 workers for 1990. While the probabilities are in general rather low, there are a number of variables which seem to be quite significant: age to some extent (up to 30 years), education (at the highest levels), industry (with agriculture and construction faring worst), occupation (administrative workers appearing to have the highest probabilities) and, finally, seniority in the job (the higher the seniority, the more likely is permanent status). Table 31 presents the detailed results from this exercise.

On the whole, the figures suggest that most new employees are hired under fixed-term contracts. While some are able to escape from that situation, especially if they have skills, a large pool of workers remain on fixed-term contracts for quite a long time (moving between jobs because of the temporal restriction of three years on the maximum tenure of fixed-term contracts and, understandably, after interim periods in unemployment). Because of their rather low cost of dismissal, they provide a shock absorber for firms to adjust their workforces should economic conditions require them to do so.

Table 31.   Probability of achieving a permanent contract status for new jobholders,[1] Spain, 1987 and 1990

	1987				1990			
	Coefficient	t	Probability	Difference of probability	Coefficient	t	Probability	Difference of probability
Reference individual	0.45	2.60	39.0		1.70	8.98	15.4	
Age								
16-19	0.17	1.73	35.0	−4.0	0.14	1.17	13.6	−1.8
25-29	−0.05	−0.46	40.2	1.2	−0.33	−3.12	20.1	4.7
30-34	−0.15	−1.07	42.7	3.7	−0.11	−0.78	16.9	1.5
35-39	−0.24	−1.42	44.8	5.7	−0.08	−0.46	16.5	1.1
40-44	0.08	0.42	37.2	−1.8	−0.20	−0.99	18.1	2.7
45-54	0.08	0.46	37.1	−1.9	−0.26	−1.36	19.0	3.6
55 +	0.17	0.74	35.1	−3.9	0.08	0.30	14.4	−1.0
Gender								
Female	0.00	0.04	38.9	−0.1	0.15	1.49	13.6	−1.8
Position within household								
Household head	−0.25	−1.53	45.2	6.2	−0.46	−2.68	22.3	7.0
Spouse	0.04	0.21	38.0	−1.0	−0.19	−0.94	18.0	2.7
Other	−0.33	−2.35	47.2	8.2	−0.31	−2.04	19.9	4.5
Civil status								
Married	0.09	0.63	36.8	−2.2	0.30	1.81	11.9	−3.5
Other	0.30	1.24	32.2	−6.8	0.26	1.09	12.2	−3.1
Level of education								
Illiterate	0.48	1.86	28.5	−10.6	0.10	0.34	14.1	−1.2
Without study	0.11	0.82	36.5	−2.5	0.28	1.67	12.1	−3.3
Upper primary	−0.04	−0.42	39.9	0.9	0.09	0.83	14.3	−1.1
Secondary	−0.06	−0.41	40.4	1.4	−0.21	−1.40	18.3	2.9
Lower vocational training	0.23	1.40	33.7	−5.3	0.31	1.82	11.8	−3.6
Upper vocational training	0.08	0.43	37.2	−1.8	−0.06	−0.32	16.1	0.8
Lower university	0.01	0.07	38.7	−0.3	−0.39	−2.06	21.1	5.7
Higher university	0.27	1.17	32.9	−6.2	−0.41	−1.97	21.5	6.1
Occupations								
Professional/technical	0.18	0.94	34.9	−4.1	−0.16	−0.88	17.6	2.3
Clerical	−0.15	−1.11	42.7	3.7	−0.45	−3.08	22.1	6.7
Sales	−0.34	−2.20	47.4	8.4	−0.21	−1.29	18.4	3.0
Service workers	−0.31	−2.55	46.7	7.7	−0.27	−1.94	19.2	3.8
Agricultural workers	0.71	2.56	23.9	−15.2	−0.19	−0.55	18.0	2.6
Industries								
Agriculture	0.31	1.09	32.0	−7.1	0.33	0.97	11.6	−3.8
Mining	−0.20	−0.92	43.9	4.9	0.15	0.68	13.5	−1.9
Metal manufacturing	0.19	0.99	34.6	−4.5	0.07	0.34	14.5	−0.9
Other manufacturing industries	0.14	0.92	35.8	−3.2	0.09	0.56	14.2	−1.2
Construction	0.38	2.53	30.4	−8.6	0.48	2.89	10.1	−5.3
Trade/hotels	0.46	3.80	28.7	−10.3	0.20	1.51	13.0	−2.4
Transport/communications	0.17	0.84	34.9	−4.1	0.16	0.75	13.4	−1.9
Services	0.20	0.95	34.4	−4.6	0.47	2.56	10.2	−5.1

Table 31 (cont.)

	1987				1990			
	Coefficient	t	Probability	Difference of probability	Coefficient	t	Probability	Difference of probability
Situation one year earlier								
Available not searching	-0.37	-1.55	48.1	9.1	-0.37	-1.28	20.8	5.5
Military service	-0.80	-5.05	58.8	19.7	-0.01	-0.06	15.5	0.1
Studying	-0.36	-3.31	47.8	8.8	0.00	-0.04	15.4	0.1
Other	-0.53	-4.83	52.2	13.2	-0.69	-6.05	26.5	11.1
Public/private sector								
Public sector	0.34	2.89	31.3	-7.7	0.04	0.36	14.8	-0.6
Job seniority								
4-6 months	-0.78	-10.02	58.2	19.2	-0.36	-4.07	20.7	5.3
7-9 months	-1.03	-10.81	64.1	25.1	-0.74	-7.82	27.5	12.1
10-12 months	-1.50	-12.73	74.2	35.2	-1.02	-8.83	33.6	18.2
Regions ("Autonomous Communities")								
País Vasco	0.53	3.20	27.5	-11.6	0.32	1.97	11.7	-3.7
Castilla-La Mancha	0.17	1.20	35.1	-3.9	0.78	4.40	7.7	-7.7
Comunidad Valenciana	0.81	6.13	22.1	-16.9	0.77	5.28	7.8	-7.6
Murcia	1.03	4.74	18.6	-20.4	0.97	3.39	6.5	-8.9
Extremadura	0.28	1.69	32.6	-6.4	-0.16	-1.00	17.5	2.1
Baleares	0.00	0.01	39.0	-0.1	0.81	2.75	7.5	-7.9
La Rioja	2.84	5.37	3.6	-35.4	1.00	2.80	6.3	-9.1
Madrid	-0.57	-3.58	53.0	14.0	-0.78	-5.79	28.3	13.0
Ceuta/Melilla	5.65	0.22	0.2	-38.8	0.10	0.23	14.1	-1.3
Cantabria	0.89	2.80	20.7	-18.3	0.49	1.76	10.0	-5.3
Canarias	0.80	5.92	22.4	-16.6	0.58	3.22	9.2	-6.1
Castilla y León	0.53	3.99	27.3	-11.7	0.78	5.01	7.7	-7.7
Navarra	0.34	1.41	31.4	-7.6	0.11	0.43	14.0	-1.4
Asturias	0.43	2.02	29.4	-9.7	0.40	1.78	10.8	-4.6
Cataluña	0.88	6.97	21.0	-18.0	1.10	7.27	5.7	-9.7
Galicia	-0.16	-0.96	43.0	3.9	0.52	2.98	9.8	-5.6
Aragón	0.40	2.25	30.1	-8.9	-0.67	-4.09	26.1	10.7

1 Employees who entered employment within the 12 months preceding the survey date.

Sample sizes: 1987: 4,836; 1990: 6,256.
Likelihood ratio test: 1987: 703; 1990: 554.

Characteristics of reference individual:
— 20-24 years old   — male
— child of household head   — single
— lower primary education   — non-agricultural production worker
— other services   — job searching a year earlier
— private sector employee   — job seniority 0-3 months
— works in Andalucía

Source: Authors' logit model.

Firings costs and job creation

After reviewing the legal regulation of Spanish employment contracts, one can discuss the degree of (employment) "flexibility" allowed for such regulation. In fact, as already commented, the controversy over the "flexibility" of the labour market has centred, in Spain, on the importance of firing restrictions which, it is claimed, were much tougher than in other countries due to the "paternalistic" legislation of the Franco era. Although this may be true in some cases, if one considers only the legal aspects of dismissals, it is less clear when one analyses the role of the labour unions and collective bargaining practices, severely restricted in Spain before 1977, and only beginning to normalize after 1980. The reform of fixed-term employment contracts is also subject to this type of discussion. It is often argued that this reform made the labour market more "flexible" allowing the employment recovery of the 1985-90 period. Thus, one popular explanation of both the employment crisis (1975-85) and the employment recovery (1986-90) relies on employment flexibility. Because of the "high rigidity" of employment arrangements during the later period, employers did not find it profitable to hire new workers. After the "flexibilization" in 1984, hirings became profitable and, hence, employment soared.

We have disputed this claim on several grounds. First, we have argued that the labour market during the 1975-85 period was not as rigid as is often claimed. We have also argued that the reasons for the employment crisis of the 1975-85 period have structural causes derived from the weakness of the Spanish economy at that time (see Chapter 1). We now discuss the effects of dismissal costs on the employers' hiring decision, to assess to what extent firing costs are an important determinant of it. We will first present a brief review of some theoretical models aimed at establishing the effects of firing costs on job creation.

There are two reasons why firing costs affect hirings. If workers were homogeneous, the expected cost of hiring a new worker includes the expected cost of firing them in case of a decrease in labour productivity. In addition, when workers are not homogeneous and their ability is unknown at the moment of hiring, the probability of hiring a low ability worker is an important component of the expected probability of a future dismissal. We now analyse the importance of these considerations, presenting simple versions of some theoretical models.

From a theoretical point of view, the effects of firing costs on the firm's hiring decision is a controversial issue. It is obvious that, as with any adjustment costs, firing costs affect the variability of employment over the business cycle (since firings are smaller in recessions and hirings are smaller during booms relative to the case of zero firing costs). But they are not necessarily decisive for the average level of hirings and the long-run average level of employment. Recent models on the effects of firing costs are not conclusive on these issues. Bentolila and Bertola (1991) present a model of firing costs where the magnitude of severance payments has only a small effect on hiring and thus on long-run average employment. On the contrary, Saint-Paul (1990) shows that the existence of firing costs combined with a low and pro-cyclical rate of voluntary departures could cause "a high unemployment trap" (proving the conjecture advanced in Blanchard and Summers,

1988). Bentolila and Saint-Paul (1992) look at the dynamics of aggregate employment after the introduction of fixed-term employment contracts. Obviously, the values of the main parameters of these models (discount rates, transition probabilities across States, magnitude of firing costs, departure rates) are crucial in determining the final effects on employment. Below, we present a simple model to illustrate the importance of these parameter values and present "back-of-envelope" calculations that suggest that in Spain the effects on employment are not large.

Suppose an employer is considering hiring a worker at a cost $w + h$, where w is the wage and $h > 0$ is the hiring cost. After a worker is hired, it costs $f > 0$ to fire her. The profit from employing a worker is a random variable which follows a binomial random distribution, that is, with probability p, times are good and profits (net of wages) are π. With probability $1 - p$, times are bad and there are losses equal to l. Workers voluntarily quit with probability δ. There are two periods. At period one, "times are good" and the employer considers hiring a new worker. At period two, when "times are bad", the worker will be fired as long as $f < l$. If $f > l$, that is, if the marginal cost of adjusting employment is greater than the loss per worker employed, the worker is not fired. This illustrates the other effect of firing costs on employment, namely, the reduction in the number of firings during recessions and, consequently, the less variability of aggregate employment over the cycle. If times are good, the employer would keep the worker, if she does not voluntarily quit. Hence, the hiring decision should depend on whether

$$(1 + \frac{p(1-\delta)}{1+r})\pi - h - (\frac{(1-p)(1-\delta)}{1+r})\min(f,l) \geq 0$$

where r is the discount rate. The left-hand side of this inequality represents the expected profits from hiring a worker at period one. It is obvious that the firing costs, f, are not the only variable affecting the hiring decision. The variability of profits across the cycle (the relationship between π and l), the probability of times being good or bad, the discount rate and the workers' voluntary quit rate also affect the hiring decision. The effect of firing costs on the number of hirings depend on all these variables. Additionally, the longer the expected duration of boom times, the less important firing costs are for hiring decisions. For illustrative purposes, suppose that the time period in the previous example is one year, the annual discount rate is 5 per cent, and losses per worker during recession are 5 times profits per worker ($l/\pi = 5$), unplausibly high but unfavourable to the point we are trying to emphasize. Figure 29 plots the value of the *ex ante* expected profits from hiring a worker (the left-hand side of the inequality above) for different values of the probability of recession and the quit rate. As the figure shows, firing costs have to be very high to restrict hirings.

On the other hand, Saint-Paul (1990) shows that an interesting possibility arises. If quit rates are pro-cyclical, it is theoretically possible to generate a "high unemployment trap". Suppose that the labour supply curve is decreasing when quits are plotted against unemployment, since workers quit their jobs more easily when unemployment is low (locus SS in figure 30). Additionally, labour demand is decreasing along the same axes, because firing costs are less important when the

Figure 29. **Ex ante** *expected profits from hiring a worker*

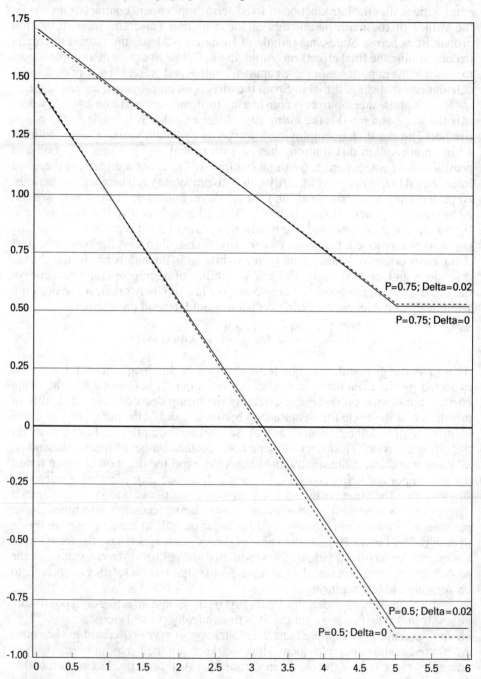

Figure 30. A "high unemployment trap"

Unemployment rate

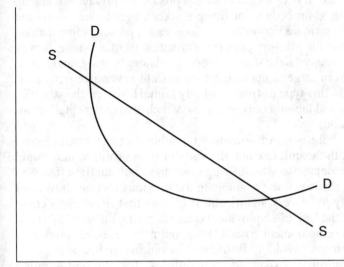

Quit rate

quit rate is high (as the simple example presented above shows). This is the locus DD in figure 30. Along this locus the wage is constant. Wage increases shift the curve to the right. As shown in the figure, there exists the possibility of two equilibria, one of them a "high unemployment trap".

Employment adjustment costs in Spain

As illustrated in the above example, firing costs per worker, that is, the marginal costs, are the relevant variable for the employer when considering firing a worker. However, the relevant variable for the hiring decision is the *ex ante* expected average cost of adjusting the labour force. This cost is related to the magnitude of the firing cost; but other variables such as the voluntary quit rate, the expected duration of the job and the discount rate also affect it. Hence, the magnitude of the effects of firing costs on aggregate employment becomes an empirical question, as these effects depend on the values of the parameters described above. The basic argument against firing costs, that is, that they affect the employer's hiring decision and so imply a lower labour demand the higher these costs, may not be the whole story; the magnitude of the other variables which affect *ex ante* employment adjustment costs may be equally important.

The available data do not allow a precise calculation of the costs of adjusting employment in the Spanish economy. However, there is some evidence that these costs are not particularly high. Legal severance payments are, in most cases, similar to those in most Western European countries, and most dismissed workers receive severance payments inferior to those stipulated by law, since there exists the possibility of agreement between employers and workers without court intervention. This adds an element of "flexibility" in the firing process which is not always fully appreciated. It is significant that this procedure, private agreement, is the most commonly used procedure for firing workers. Fernández, Muro and Toharia (1988) and Ministerio de Economía (various years) present some data on average firing costs. While the Ministry obtains information from an annual survey of large firms, the former analyses the statistics for conciliatory hearings and labour court decisions. Data from large firms suggest significant severance payments, since average seniority in this type of firm is usually high. However, the statistics on conciliatory hearings and labour court decisions, which also cover small firms, give a different impression.

Unfortunately, there is no information available on the magnitude and cyclical behaviour of both the quit rate and the variability of profits which would allow us to quantify the degree to which firing costs have substantial effects on firms' hiring decisions. However, the example in the previous section shows that these effects are unlikely to be very significant. It follows that firing costs could not be the main cause of the lack of employment creation during the late 1970s and early 1980s that led to the employment crisis. On the contrary, these costs obviously reduced firings at that time, so avoiding further reductions in employment.

For similar reasons, expanded possibilities for limited-duration employment arrangements (involving substantially lower firing costs) are not likely to affect hirings significantly (if firms behave rationally). Hence, the legal reforms that facilitated this sort of contract cannot be the main cause of the recovery of employment in Spain in the latter 1980s. Some authors claim that the great success of such contractual forms is proof of their utility and beneficial effects on employment. This claim is obviously wrong. The fact that employers mostly use fixed-term employment contracts means only that it is more profitable to do so than to hire under permanent contracts. It does not mean that hirings under permanent contracts are unprofitable and that they would have not occurred in the event of restrictions on fixed-term employment contracts. Without knowing how employment would have evolved in the absence of the 1984 reforms, it is difficult to ascertain how important the easing restrictions were for employment creation. But the same reasoning as for firing costs leads us to conclude that they were not very important.

Another argument also suggests that employment flexibility has not been an important factor in creating employment. In the description of the sectoral evolution of employment in Chapter 1, we stressed the employment shifts in construction and, in particular, the large decrease in employment that this sector suffered during the employment crisis. This sector, by nature, is one where temporary labour contracts can be and are used freely (see table 27). Had employment rigidities been an important factor in the hiring decision and the main cause of lack of employment creation, we would have observed a better performance by a sector like construction, where employment flexibility is greater.

Other effects of fixed-term employment contracts

Despite the controversial effects of firing costs on job creation, the fact is that the Spanish law opted for "flexibilization" of the labour market. And it did so in a peculiar way: reducing the job security of new entrants into employment (if they were hired under fixed-term contracts) without reducing the job security of those already employed under permanent full-time contracts. For the reasons presented in the previous section, the employment effects of this "flexibilization" are difficult to ascertain and, thus, subject of some debate. One attempt at measuring these effects is in Bentolila and Saint-Paul (1992), who estimate that the reform of fixed-term contracts contributed to increased employment by 1.5 per cent during a three-year period. In any case, besides these employment effects, this "flexibilization" strategy has had other interesting effects on the labour market, which we will now discuss.

First, it must be realized that a segmentation of the labour market between permanent and fixed-term employment has arisen. This segmentation has important implications since not only employment, but also labour productivity, wages and turnover rates are clearly related to the degree to which fixed-term employment contracts are used.

There are two reasons why the huge increase of fixed-term employment may have had an effect on labour productivity. The first has to do with the relationship between the form of the employment contract and employees' motivation or willingness to exert effort (these are called "efficiency effects" by Jimeno and Toharia, 1991b). The second reason arises from the coexistence of permanent workers and workers employed under fixed-term contracts ("cooperation effects").[4] The "efficiency effects" of fixed-term employment on labour productivity could be positive or negative. Positive effects may arise if temporary workers perceive that the chances of gaining permanent status depend on their job performance. On the other hand, if that probability is low, in any case, the average productivity of temporary workers would be also low (see Jimeno and Toharia, 1991c). "Cooperation effects" determine the marginal productivity of temporary workers. If this marginal productivity were constant, we would observe that, in steady state, firms employ workers under only one type of contract — permanent or limited duration — depending on whether "efficiency effects" are positive or negative. The fact that firms employ both of these indicates that the type of contract has an effect on the marginal productivity of labour.

The expansion of fixed-term employment in Spain offers some evidence on the importance of these productivity effects. Although the availability of data does not permit a very precise test, Jimeno and Toharia (1991b) give a cross-sectional analysis that suggests the existence of a negative correlation between the two variables, which persists after controlling for the changes in labour composition that the increase in fixed-term employment has generated.

With respect to wages, there are two reasons why the development of fixed-term employment is important. First, the segmentation of the labour market caused by the widespread use of fixed-term employment contracts has important implications for the dynamics of wage setting, particularly when wages are mainly determined by collective bargaining, as in Spain. For instance, if worker representatives in collective bargaining are permanent workers who care less about the concerns of workers employed under fixed-term contracts, there would be upward pressure on wages. Permanent workers would perceive that their jobs were relatively secure because of the existence of temporary workers within the firm who would be fired first if wage increases were excessive.[5] Secondly, workers employed under fixed-term contracts have less legal protection, and this could open the way for the employer to practise discrimination (although discrimination in wage rates could be forbidden).

The Spanish evidence supports the existence of these wage effects of fixed-term employment. A cross-sectional analysis of wage rates shows a positive correlation between wage increases and fixed-term employment. As a counterbalance, there is also evidence of wage discrimination against temporary workers. Data from a survey on earnings carried out as part of the *Labour Force Survey* show that, after controlling for observable personal characteristics, workers employed under fixed-term contracts earn approximately 10 per cent less than permanent workers (Jimeno and Toharia, 1991b). Furthermore, Bentolila and Dolado (1992) have estimated that a one percentage point increase in the proportion of fixed-term employment raises the growth rate of permanent workers' wages by one-third of a percentage point.

Finally, turnover rates have increased substantially as a result of the growth of fixed-term employment. As already noted, by law this type of contract has to be converted into a permanent contract after three years. Thus, turnover rates increase when enterprises employ workers under fixed-term contracts and achieve an optimal composition of their labour force by successive firing and hiring. This, in principle, is a positive effect of fixed-term employment since it reduces average unemployment duration. However, in the Spanish case, it has had perverse effects on the budget deficit through an increase in unemployment compensation. The Spanish unemployment system (described in the next chapter) requires contributions for a certain period before workers are entitled to unemployment benefit. These contributions can be paid only while the worker is employed. As turnover rates have increased and more people have gained job experience, entitlements to unemployment benefit have also increased. The government responses have been, first, to raise by 1 per cent the social security contributions paid by employers (which will have a negative effect on total employment) and, afterwards, in April 1992, to modify the amount, duration and entitlement requirements of unemployment subsidies (see Chapter 5).

Concluding remarks

In this chapter, we have reviewed one of the most important developments in Spanish labour markets during recent years, that is, the "flexibilization" of the labour market, consisting in the reform of fixed-term employment contracts. This reform has resulted in a huge increase of employment under this type of contract. The analysis of the incidence of fixed-term employment contracts shows that they are becoming the main norm of entrance into the labour market and that the conversion rates into permanent employment are low. We have also suggested that the positive employment effects of fixed-term contracts are doubtful, and that there are additional effects on labour productivity, wages and turnover rates which should be considered in a full analysis of these policies. The Spanish experience shows that recourse to labour market "flexibilization" through the promotion of fixed-term employment could have substantial implications for (the variability of) employment, although not necessarily for its average level through the business cycle, and could also involve costs which would by no means be negligible.

Notes

[1] See Emerson (1988).

[2] See Malo de Molina (1984 and 1985).

[3] For a summary of the different positions, see Malo de Molina (1988).

[4] This type of effect has been stressed in the "insider-outsider" literature (see Lindberg and Snower, 1988).

[5] This assumes that, as in Spain, discrimination in wage rates is not permitted.

Chapter 5

Unemployment and labour market policy: Past, present and future

It is useful to disentangle to what extent the unemployment protection system ... favours the "subsidy culture" instead of the "sacrifice and hard-work culture". It can be discussed whether unemployment benefits constitute passive (employment) policy or whether they contain some element of active policy ... First, it must be recalled that, in many cases, unemployment benefits are related to participation in training programmes. Second, in a good number of cases, unemployment benefits avoid making workers redundant from enterprises in difficulty, by totally or partly financing their wages during a determined period. ... Finally, in many cases, unemployment benefits are no more than a way of translating to public finances some of the labour costs of the enterprises, and, under these circumstances, they can be labelled as public incentives to employment. Thus, these arguments lead to the view that the difference between active and passive employment policies are not so clearcut ... and that our system can be classified either as one of unemployment protection or also as one that subsidizes employment.

(Translation from *La reforma de las políticas de fomento del empleo y de protección por desempleo* [The reform of employment promotion and unemployment protection policies], Ministerio de Trabajo y de Seguridad Social, Apr. 1992.)

Introduction

Unemployment arises when people look for a job and cannot find one. Though a tautology, this is a good starting point to understanding the causes of unemployment and the possible policy options to tackle it. There are three reasons why jobs might not be available for those seeking work:

    (i)   hirings are restricted by prevailing demand conditions, wages and/or legal regulation of employment conditions,

    (ii) job vacancies are available but people are not able (or willing) to find them, and

    (iii) job vacancies are available but the unemployed do not have the skills needed to fill them.

With this simple characterization of the causes of unemployment, we can classify labour market policies into three categories:

Table 32.   *Public expenditure on labour market programmes as a percentage of GDP in several OECD countries (average 1986-89)*

	Public employment services and administration	Labour market training	Youth measures	Subsidized employment	Measures for the disabled	Unemployment compensation	Early retirement	Total
Spain	0.10	0.08	0.06	0.47	0.01 [1]	2.35	0.05	3.20
France	0.12	0.29	0.25	0.05	0.05	1.28	0.84	2.90
Germany (Fed. Rep.)	0.23	0.30	0.05	0.20	0.22	1.30	0.02	2.32
Italy [2]	0.09	0.02	0.64	–	–	0.49	0.31	1.55
Japan [3]	0.03	0.03	–	0.11	0.01	0.39	–	0.60
Sweden	0.23	0.51	0.10	0.22	0.75	0.65	0.10	2.56
United Kingdom	0.15	0.15	0.24	0.20	0.03	1.61	0.01	2.14
United States	0.07	0.11	0.03	0.01	0.04	0.49	–	0.76

[1] Average 1986-88. [2] Italy, average 1986-88. [3] Japan, average 1987-89.
Source: OECD, 1991, note B.

(i)   policies aimed at stimulating labour demand by creating jobs, retaining existing jobs by reducing labour costs, or reforming legal institutions,

(ii) reform of the unemployment protection and tax systems to eliminate possible perverse effects on the willingness of unemployed people to accept job offers, and

(iii) employment and training programmes designed to enhance the skills of unemployed persons and minimize the mismatch between labour supply and demand.

We use this classification to review the labour market policies pursued in Spain in the 15 years to 1990 and to offer some options for the future that we believe are worth consideration. As a general comment, we can say that Spain belongs to that group of countries where "active" labour market policies are taken to be subsidiary to traditional demand management policies. Although public expenditure on labour market policies in Spain is, as a percentage of GDP, among the highest in OECD countries (see table 32), most of that expenditure is on income maintenance programmes.[1] In fact, the expenditure on "active measures" (first five columns in the table) has been only around 0.71 per cent of GDP, in marked contrast to countries like the Federal Republic of Germany and Sweden. Regarding the evolution of "active" labour market policies and the Government's response to the unemployment problem that arose during the 1975-85 employment crisis, the reform of employment contracts in 1984 was the main innovation in the past decade and a half. Other "active" labour market policies have had a "passive" role (despite the claim contained in the quotation at the beginning of this chapter), meaning that they were aimed at easing crisis situations rather than anticipating the difficulties of the unemployed in finding jobs and trying to help them to solve the causes of those difficulties.

The reform of employment contracts as an employment promotion policy

Besides the traditional recipes for stimulating the economy using fiscal and monetary measures, more direct approaches can be pursued to increase the demand for labour. Among these, the use of employment subsidies and the creation of new contractual employment forms have been predominant in Spain.[2] Although we have already discussed the evolution and incidence of fixed-term employment contracts and their effects (see Chapter 4), we now describe the reforms of employment contracts in more detail. We then analyse the existing programmes aimed at subsidizing employment creation.

Among the types of fixed-term employment contract described in Chapter 4, the most relevant for employment policy is the so-called "contract for the promotion of employment" [*contrato de fomento del empleo*]. The rationale for its introduction was to provide more "flexibility" to employers when adjusting their labour force and, therefore, to encourage employment creation in a situation of depressed labour demand (as in 1984, when restrictions on the use of this type of contract were lifted) *without* reducing the job security of those already employed. As employers made extensive use of this type of contract, fixed-term employment increased very rapidly (see Chapter 4). This experience constitutes the basic argument of those who favour this type of flexibilization policy since, they point out, the proof that these contracts are successful is that they are widely used. Here, we review to what extent this specific type of contract is used. The following analysis is based on data on labour markets flows provided by the National Institute for Employment [*Instituto Nacional de Empleo* or INEM] and draws also on Segura et al. (1991).

For this analysis, we shall distinguish between three types of fixed-term employment contract: (i) "contracts for the promotion of employment" (CPE), (ii) "training contracts" (TrC) and (iii) temporary contracts (TempC) justified by the seasonality of the job or the economic activity of the firm. Table 33 presents the number of these contracts registered in the INEM since 1984, when employers started to used them regularly. As the table shows, fixed-term contracts of the first two types (promotion of employment and training) have increased significantly both in number and as a proportion of the total, while the percentage of temporary contracts justified by the economic activity of the firm has decreased.

For some authors, the development of fixed-term contracts for the "promotion of employment" and training suggests that "flexibilization" policies have increased labour market efficiency (see, for instance, Espina, 1991). However, one has to be careful in associating the number of new fixed-term contracts with employment creation. As already argued in Chapter 4, the use of these contracts indicates only that it is more profitable for employers to hire workers under these contracts than under the typical permanent one, and not necessarily that hirings would have been lower had these "contracts for the promotion of employment" not been available.[3] Additionally, the segmentation of the labour market resulting from these policies may have had negative effects on productivity and wage determination, as argued in Chapter 4. Hence, it is a moot point whether the Spanish

Table 33.   Fixed-term employment contracts by type, Spain, 1984-89

	1984	1985	1986	1987	1988	1989
Number						
CPE	235 368	432 175	536 594	666 577	862 400	1 100 371
TrC	41 412	164 502	247 797	346 416	433 832	553 995
TempC	1 459 891	1 470 040	1 795 319	2 109 129	2 453 746	2 761 530
%						
CPE	13.6	20.9	20.8	21.4	23.0	24.9
TrC	2.4	8.0	9.6	11.1	11.5	12.5
TempC	84.1	71.1	69.6	67.6	65.4	62.5

Source: Segura et al., 1991, CPE: Contracts for the promotion of employment; TrC: training contracts; TempC: temporary contracts.

experience shows that "flexibilization" policies based on the introduction of fixed-term employment contracts are wholly desirable.

Employment subsidies, public employment and work-sharing

For our purposes, it is convenient to separate government interventions in the labour market involving some kind of employment subsidy into two classes:

(i)   measures aimed at avoiding job losses, and

(ii) measures to provide incentives for the creation of new jobs.

In Spain, there are three types of measures aimed at avoiding job losses. First, there are special provisions for sectors in crisis, which aim to reduce the costs of moving financial and human resources to other, healthier sectors. These are administered through two main institutions:

(a)   *employment promotion funds,* financed by employers' and workers' contributions and subsidies from public and private organizations. Resources are mainly directed to supplement the unemployment benefits of redundant workers and to encourage the creation of alternative employment; and

(b)   *urgent re-industrialization zones,* geographical zones where employment in sectors in crisis is relatively important. They are declared "priority zones" (in regard to job creation) by the central Government, after agreement with the local authorities, and qualify for subsidies, fiscal benefits (direct or through special investment depreciation plans) and credits at favourable interest rates. The costs are financed directly through the government budget.

The second type of measures aimed at avoiding job losses takes the form of subsidies to labour cooperatives and workplaces employing disabled workers. Table 34, which presents data on the number of cooperatives and workers

Table 34.   Number of workers'cooperatives and their members, Spain, 1985-91

Year	Number of workers' cooperatives	Members
1985	1 406	11 715
1986	2 119	17 654
1987	1 639	12 744
1988	1 471	10 969
1989	1 203	8 499
1990	964	6 642
1991	937	6 261

Note: Excludes cooperatives in the País Vasco [Basque Country].
Source: *Boletín de Estadísticas Laborales.*

associated with them, shows that the cooperative movement is not a big source of job creation in Spain, despite anecdotal cases sometimes taken as examples in the industrial relations literature, such as Mondragón, no doubt interesting for other reasons. Thus, the employment effects of this type of programme are negligible. It is also interesting to note the countercyclical behaviour of the number and members of labour cooperatives (both variables decreased very significantly during the period of recovery of employment), a similar evolution to that followed by self-employment.

Finally, firms within sectors in crisis can temporarily lay off part of their workforce or reduce daily working hours until economic conditions improve. Workers affected by this type of measure are entitled to receive unemployment benefits. As a general rule, the firm affected contributes towards financing these benefits. Table 35 presents some figures on the number of workers affected by temporary lay-offs. These numbers represent less than 2 per cent of wage and salary earners (in recent years); in 1984, this percentage was close to 6 per cent. The argument for temporary lay-offs and short-time working depends on the characteristics of the adverse shocks affecting the industry in question. If these shocks are transitory, the measures may be justified, although it is important that the firm share some of the costs. Otherwise, they would have an incentive to make excessive use of temporary lay-offs as an easy way to cut costs.

The incentives for the creation of new jobs are many and take different forms. A secondary role is played by employment programmes in the public sector, which hire unemployed people for public works. They are carried out by local governments in collaboration with INEM, which normally finances between 40 per cent and 75 per cent of the labour costs. An important part of this type of programme is the *Plan de Empleo Rural* [Rural Employment Plan] which affects agricultural workers (and may be an important cause of reduced migration from traditional zones of emigration such as Andalucía and Extremadura). Other instruments aimed at job creation are the subsidies for new business initiatives, mostly designed to encourage unemployed persons to become self-employed. Those willing to start a new business can receive all the unemployment benefits to

Table 35.   Workers affected by temporary lay-offs by broad sectors, Spain, 1979-91

Year	Total number of firms	Total number of workers	Industry	Construction	Services
1979	n.a.	152 471	99 965	17 186	15 929
1980	n.a.	256 675	182 043	26 203	33 109
1981	n.a.	240 894	169 587	13 124	29 619
1982	6 560	239 473	151 818	15 795	54 597
1983	9 305	369 815	272 797	8 861	66 281
1984	7 720	407 453	342 803	6 185	36 515
1985	7 914	362 351	289 003	4 764	42 411
1986	8 017	259 919	208 073	2 633	24 749
1987	6 346	230 786	179 014	2 297	30 419
1988	5 853	214 121	166 001	1 755	20 988
1989	4 696	214 121	107 231	1 150	12 557
1990	5 010	257 033	215 664	3 179	15 997
1991	5 812	213 744	163 640	995	25 410

Source: *Boletín de Estadísticas Laborales,* variousl issues.

Table 36.   Workers who have capitalized their unemployment benefits to become self-employed, Spain, 1985-91

1985 (September-December)	16 848
1986	59 240
1987	64 192
1988	74 827
1989	82 097
1990	76 451
1991	81 513

Source: *Boletín de Estadísticas Laborales*, various issues.

which they are entitled in advance as a capital sum and obtain subsidized credits. Table 36 presents the number of workers enrolled in this programme in recent years which has been increasing but has remained small. In April 1992, this programme was discontinued, as part of the Government's reform of the unemployment insurance system (which we will discuss below).

Another alternative which is often proposed to create employment is work-sharing. However, the effectiveness of work-sharing in reducing unemployment is not proven, although it is a policy which is often proposed. Layard, Nickell and Jackman (1991, Chapter 10) argue that work-sharing is, at best, inflationary (since it initially reduces unemployment but this is translated into price increases) and, at worst, ineffective in reducing unemployment in the long run (when the Government is not willing to accommodate the increase in inflation).[4] In addition, when non-wage labour costs are important, the reduction of hours per worker together with a proportional increase in the number of workers increases total labour costs.

Hence, to impose binding restrictions on the number of hours does not seem a sensible policy.

In the Spanish case, the most important legal provisions affecting working hours are not particularly "rigid". On the contrary, working hours are mostly determined by collective bargaining, although there are some constraints imposed by the law, the most important being:

(i)   a maximum of 40 weekly working hours,

(ii) a minimum vacation of 30 working days,

(iii) a maximum number of overtime hours of 80 per year, paid at a premium of at least 75 per cent over wages for normal hours.

Thus, as already mentioned in Chapter 3, there is considerable flexibility for employers and workers to determine working hours by collective bargaining. Another question is to what extent this flexibility is used to determine hours with work-sharing as a goal. There are in fact some reasons to think that employers' and/or workers' representatives in collective bargaining have some interest in work-sharing. For instance, of the 253 collective agreements signed in 1990 whose geographical scope was larger than a region (*autonomous community*), 77 imposed some kind of limitation on overtime work. Thus, 55 collective agreements prohibited *normal* reliance on overtime (as opposed to structural overtime caused by unforeseen circumstances). Additionally, 26 collective agreements established that newly hired workers would not be allowed to do *structural* overtime. Moreover, it is also possible to remunerate overtime hours with additional vacation days (this is contained in 20 of the 253 collective agreements), although this form of remuneration is generally used in combination with the more usual monetary compensation. Most rare are additional limitations on the maximum number of overtime hours (only one agreement lowered to 60 hours the legal restriction of 80 overtime hours per worker per year).[5]

Part-time employment is not an important component of total Spanish employment. Part-time employment contracts are regulated on a proportional basis to the typical full-time permanent contract, meaning that they impose similar obligations (regarding collective bargaining rights, social security rights, and so on) on the employer's side. This and the important non-wage component of labour costs (see table 37) might be the main reasons why part-time contracts are not used more extensively.[6] The main difference between Spain and other EC countries is not the high proportion of non-wage costs within total labour costs (around 25 per cent, both as an average in the EC and in Spain) but the fact that, given Spanish regulations, these percentages apply equally to Spanish full-time and part-time workers while in other EC countries the non-wage component of part-time labour costs is much lower than that of full-time labour.

Finally, another way of achieving work-sharing is early retirement. In Spain, retirement is compulsory at 65 years of age. In addition, a number of early retirement schemes have been implemented at the collective bargaining level, taking advantage of a legal regulation favouring early retirement if the retiring worker is replaced by an unemployed. However, the use of these schemes has been

*Table 37.   Components of labour costs (as a percentage of total costs) in manufacturing in some
           EC countries, 1988*

	Wages	Compulsory employer's social security contributions	Voluntary employer's social security contributions	Vocational training	Taxes	Other	Subsidies
EC	75.7	17.2	5.0	1.4	–	1.3	0.7
Belgium	70.6	23.8	3.8	0.2	–	2.0	0.7
Denmark	96.4	1.9	1.2	2.0	–	0.4	2.0
Germany (Fed. Rep.)	76.4	16.6	4.8	1.5	–	0.8	0.1
France	68.3	18.4	9.5	1.9	–	1.7	–
Ireland	82.6	8.0	6.9	0.9	–	1.8	0.1
Italy	70.3	30.4	1.4	1.3	0.5	1.6	5.4
Netherlands	73.8	15.5	7.2	0.6	–	2.9	0.1
Portugal	74.0	18.7	2.9	2.9	–	1.5	–
United Kingdom	85.4	7.2	4.9	1.3	–	1.3	0.1
Spain	75.0	22.5	1.9	0.2	–	1.3	1.0

Source: *EC Labour Costs Survey.*

very limited. For instance, in 1988 the number of workers hired under them was 1,473; in 1989, 1,565; in 1990, 2,283; and in 1991, 2,611.

The unemployment protection system

The widespread availability of income maintenance is one of the most important social achievements of our times. These programmes are the main instrument of income redistribution and, therefore and not surprisingly, one of the largest components of public spending. The possible impact of unemployment benefits on the unemployment rate (because of their effects on the job-search intensity of unemployed workers and on wage determination) introduces a certain trade-off between the desirability of income support to those in need, constrained only by the resources available, and labour supply flexibility. This trade-off is the basic problem to consider when deciding the role of income maintenance in labour market policies.

As in most Western European countries, the unemployment protection system in Spain follows both the "insurance" and the "assistance" principles.[7] According to the "insurance" principle, unemployment protection should be considered an insurance mechanism and, hence, only those unemployed persons who have been employed previously and contributed to social security funds are entitled to receive unemployment compensation. As a general rule and under this principle, unemployment benefits should have a limited duration and the amount of the benefit should be related to past contributions. On the other hand, the "assistance" principle establishes that those persons in special need should receive help from the State. Since most of the unemployed are within this group, there should be an unemployment subsidy. It is important to notice that under this latter principle, the current and previous employment situation of the person is not the concept that entitles him or her to receive the unemployment subsidy but, in some specific cases, the cause of being in the special circumstances that are to be subsidized.[8]

In Spain, unlike in other Western European countries, the "assistance" principle applies jointly with the "insurance" principle, that is, only those unemployed people eligible to receive unemployment benefits can receive additional benefits under the "assistance" principle.[9] Thus, unemployed people without any employment experience (and, therefore, no record of social security contributions) are not entitled to receive unemployment benefits. This creates some confusion and contributes to increasing the duration of unemployment benefits, since some of the unemployed are entitled to receive unemployment subsidies after their eligibility period until the contribution scheme expires.

In summary, the main characteristics of the Spanish unemployment protection system are the following:[10]

(i)   The unemployment protection system covers all groups of workers, except civil servants and domestic workers.

(ii) To receive unemployment benefit, workers must have made social security contributions for a period of six (12) months during the previous four years. The amounts of benefits (replacement ratios) are as follows:

(a) 80 (70) per cent of the base wage (generally speaking, this is significantly lower than total earnings) during the first six months of the unemployment period,

(b) 70 (60) per cent of the base wage from the seventh to 12th month,

(c) 60 (50) per cent of the base wage from the 13th month,

(d) a maximum benefit limit (170 per cent to 220 per cent of the minimum wage, depending on the number of dependent children).

(iii) The duration of entitlement to unemployment benefits also depends on the number of months of past contributions (see table 38), with a maximum of two years.

(iv) Workers older than 55 years with dependants are entitled to additional benefits after unemployment insurance benefit has ceased. The compensation in this case is 75 per cent of the minimum wage. This compensation is paid for six months, which can be extended for successive six-month periods until retirement age.

(v)   A special unemployment protection programme for agricultural workers (related to the *Plan de Empleo Rural*, already mentioned) is financed exclusively by state funds. Those agricultural workers with incomes no higher than the minimum wage, who have worked at least 60 days a year, are entitled to receive benefits equal to 75 per cent of the minimum wage for six months. While this system has been criticized for its negative influence on labour mobility, as already

Table 38. ***Duration of unemployment benefits in Spain, before and after the 1992 reform.***

Contribution period (months)	Entitlement period (months)	
	Pre-reform	Post-reform
6 to 12	3	–
12 to 18	6	4
18 to 24	9	6
24 to 30	12	8
30 to 36	15	10
36 to 42	18	12
From 42	24	22

Table 39. ***Evolution of expenses on unemployment benefits and their sources (billions of pesetas), Spain, 1987-91***

Concept	1987	1988	1989	1990	1991
Benefits under the contributory scheme	599.7	664.8	739.9	902.0	1 156.2
Benefits under the assistance scheme	288.9	298.3	352.0	403.2	460.1
Total unemployment benefits	888.6	963.1	1 091.9	1 305.2	1 616.3
State funds	364.0	352.3	417.8	402.7	423.5
Social security´s (workers´and employers´) contributions	527.9	598.0	699.4	802.3	879.6
Deficit	–3.3	12.8	–25.3	100.2	313.2

Source: *La reforma de las políticas de fomento del empleo y de protección por desempleo* [The reform of employment promotion and unemployment protection policies], Ministerio de Trabajo y de Seguridad Social, Apr. 1992. Data for 1991 are provisional.

mentioned, its importance in terms of total expenditure on unemployment benefits remains rather small: some 6 per cent.

(vi) Unemployment benefits are not subject to income tax, and additional benefits are restricted to health protection similar to that provided by social security to employed workers.

The Spanish unemployment protection system has come under considerable financial strain in recent years. As table 39 clearly illustrates, expenditure on unemployment benefits, in particular those associated with the "insurance" principle, have dramatically increased after 1989. The coverage rate, whose evolution is illustrated in figure 31, has also accelerated its gently upward trend initiated in 1984. These developments can partly be linked to the widespread use of fixed-term contracts, although the "explosion" of the system in 1990-91 can hardly be traced, as both the Government and the social partners seem to believe, to a change which took place five years earlier. Partly as a result of these strains, and partly as a measure aimed at fostering the job-search activities of the unemployed, considered an important element in the persistence of unemployment — an argument to which we shall come back later in this section —the Spanish Government introduced in early 1992 a reform of the system, consisting of a

Figure 31. Percentage of unemployed people covered by the unemployment protection system, Spain, 1976-89

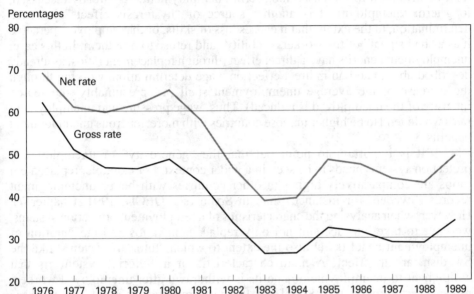

Note: The gross rate is computed from data on registered unemployment. The net rate excludes agriculture.

reduction in the benefits and an increase in the eligibility requirements. However, the main philosophy of the system, in particular the reliance on a mixture of the two principles, has remained unchanged.

The relatively low coverage rates of the unemployment protection system, despite the recent upsurge, and the modest replacement ratios — more so after the 1992 reform — lead us to conclude that the direct effects of the system on the unemployment rate (that is, the likelihood of unemployed people refusing job offers or not searching for them) are small and concentrated among special groups of workers, namely, those older than 55 years and agricultural workers, who do not in any case have many job opportunities. This conclusion is supported by the empirical evidence reported in Toharia (1991) regarding the job-search intensity of different groups of workers, defined as the ability to mention other methods of job search in addition to registration with the public employment agencies.

However, the indirect effects of low-search intensity of some unemployed workers on the unemployment rate, through their effects on wage determination, could be more important, and it appears that this view was also behind the 1992 reform. As explained by Layard, Nickell and Jackman (1991, Chapter 2) replacement ratios are one of the determinants of the "insider weight" which introduces "hysteresis effects" in wage determination.

Although, in the Spanish case, the replacement ratios are not excessively high and the entitlement to unemployment benefits is limited in time, benefits are, in general, high enough to make unemployment tolerable.[11]

An additional, supposedly perverse, effect of unemployment benefits is their contribution to increased long-term unemployment. As already discussed, long-term unemployment is another source of "hysteresis effects" in wage determination, to the extent that it causes loss of skills, or that employers perceive it as a "bad signal" of the workers' "ability" and refuse to hire them. In this case, unemployment benefits have a direct effect (through replacement ratios, as already described above) and an indirect effect on wage determination, working through the increase of the average unemployment spell (as, presumably, the search intensity of the unemployed is reduced). Thus, wage pressure and unemployment rates would tend to be higher in those countries with more generous unemployment benefits.

It is important to point out that the "generosity" of unemployment protection systems needs to be seen in a wider context. For example, replacement ratios are comparatively higher in other countries with better unemployment records (Sweden, for instance) than in Spain (see OECD, 1991, Chapter 7). However, when analysing the characteristics of unemployment protection systems, we have to take into account not only replacement ratios and the duration of unemployment benefits but also the extent to which "tutorial" systems, like the Swedish, are in effect. A main characteristic of a "tutorial system" is that entitlement to unemployment benefits is withdrawn after unemployed workers refuse a certain number of job offers. It is also important to point out that these "tutorial" systems almost always go together with a very strong participation of the state employment offices in job "broking" and placement (see OECD, 1992, Chapter 3) and the expenditure of a great deal of resources to help unemployed workers find jobs that suit them. Otherwise, this type of system would not be wholly justified.

With these caveats in mind, we can conclude that there is a positive relationship between unemployment benefits and unemployment. For instance, Burda (1988) presents some econometric evidence in support of such a relationship across OECD countries.

In the Spanish case, these considerations must be treated with some caution. As we saw in Chapter 2, long-term unemployment is mainly concentrated on young workers and women with no work experience who are, therefore, not entitled to unemployment benefits. Thus a reform of the unemployment benefit system concentrated on lowering the replacement ratios, such as that undertaken in early 1992, is bound to have little effect on the composition and level of unemployment, although it will certainly ease the financial strains of the system. More promising could be the adoption of a "tutorial system" whereby the unemployed are helped to find jobs, and unemployment benefits are denied if a certain number of reasonable available job vacancies are turned down. The 1992 reform of the unemployment protection system contains a declaration of principle which, if correctly implemented, would be equivalent to such a system. However, the role played by public employment agencies is crucial here, an issue that we discuss below.

On the whole, however, the main problem with Spain's unemployment protection system is that its two main elements, namely the insurance and the assistance benefits, are not sufficiently separated. The insurance benefits ought to be more closely related to insurance principles, whereas the assistance benefits ought to be made independent of unemployment and integrated with general social welfare policy.

Policies aimed at reducing mismatch

As is well-known, the mismatch between labour supply and demand increases unemployment. Or, in other words, the dispersion of unemployment across regions, occupations or industrial sectors is positively correlated with the level of the equilibrium unemployment rate. The reason can be explained very easily. This type of mismatch reduces labour market competition, which increases wage pressure and, thus, unemployment. Therefore, policies aimed at reducing mismatch would reduce unemployment. The reduction of labour mobility costs (or providing incentives for mobility), and the provision of training programmes to enhance the skills of unemployed workers, are the most obvious examples of this type of policy. Migration policies, in most Western European countries, are limited to making subsidies available to workers moving to a job in a different geographical location. In any case — occupational mismatch being the most important form of mismatch — those measures aimed at matching unemployed workers and existing job offers and those affecting vocational training and retraining, are the most important policy interventions.

The main task of any employment agency should be to match unemployed workers and existing job vacancies. Different countries have different methods in this regard (see, for instance, OECD, 1991, Chapter 7, and OECD, 1992, Chapter 3). In Spain, private employment agencies are not permitted, the public employment agencies of INEM being the only ones available. Whether this is the best matching system is doubtful, but more important than the ownership of employment agencies is the resources devoted to help the unemployed find jobs. The amount of these resources is the main determinant of the efficiency of employment agencies in matching unemployed workers and job vacancies. It is also usual for public employment agencies to administer the unemployment protection system. Whether they concentrate on their matching function or on this second task is another key issue to consider when looking at the effects of employment agencies on the performance of the labour market. Table 40 presents comparative European data on the number of offices and staff members in public employment services. As these figures show, Spain and Greece are, by a large margin, the countries dedicating least resources to public employment services. It is therefore not surprising that the efficiency of Spain's employment agencies in matching unemployed workers and job vacancies is extremely low. The agencies concentrate mostly on the administration of unemployment benefits.

As a consequence of their low matching efficiency, employment agencies are little used by firms to find workers to fill their vacancies. Employment agencies in Spain receive two types of job vacancy notification. For so-called "generic job offers", the agencies try to find a suitable worker. For so-called "nominative job

Table 40.   Unemployed persons per staff member in public employment services, selected European countries, 1988

Sweden	14
United Kingdom	53
Denmark	81
Germany (Fed. Rep.)	86
Netherlands	152
Canada	213
Portugal	266
France	271
Spain	712
Greece	733

Source: OECD (1991), Chapter 7.

Table 41.   "Job offers" registered with public employment agencies, Spain, 1978-91 (thousands)

	Total	"Generic"
1978	1 388.9	363.0
1979	1 657.6	555.6
1980	2 004.1	681.2
1981	2 063.4	614.6
1982	1 698.2	251.6
1983	1 557.7	200.4
1984	1 910.7	338.6
1985	2 684.0	583.1
1986	3 167.3	629.3
1987	3 610.0	647.1
1988	3 902.0	721.3
1989	4 527.9	762.3
1990	5 336.9	684.4
1991	5 226.4	599.6

Source: *Boletín de estadísticas laborales*, various issues.

offers" (where the firm proposes the worker to fill the vacancy), the intervention of the employment agency is limited to registering the corresponding employment contract. Table 41 presents data on notifications of job vacancies received by public employment agencies in recent years distinguishing these two types. As can be seen from the table, most "job offers" are of the second type.

The other important aspect of policies against mismatch refers to training for the unemployed. The general principles governing the design of the vocational training system in Spain are contained in the *Plan Nacional de Formación e Inserción Profesional (Plan FIP)* [National Plan on Vocational Training and Entry into Working Life], approved in 1985 in an effort to provide an adequate planning effort for the aid that was to become available with the accession of Spain into the European Community. These principles are:[12]

    (i)   to guarantee compatibility between the skills of the labour force and the requirements of the productive system,

    (ii) to use vocational training and employment policies as joint instruments to combat long-term unemployment,

    (iii) to coordinate the interventions of central and local Government, and

    (iv) to promote the participation of the social partners (employers and workers) in the design of vocational training plans.

Following these general principles, there is a special emphasis on the needs of those groups encountering the biggest problems of employment integration, such as youth, women workers and the long-term unemployed. The main instrument of the *Plan FIP* is the offer of training courses (and grants aimed at covering their expenses) to the unemployed, under the auspices of INEM.

Theoretically, the case for this type of policy is obvious (reducing mismatch reduces unemployment), although some have claimed that excessive emphasis on them (again, Sweden is a good example) may contribute to increased wage pressure.[13] What would seem a bad strategy would be the introduction of these policies without identifying the mismatch and the nature of the training courses needed to solve the problem, in particular in terms of the adequate balance between classroom and on-the-job training. Unfortunately, this may have been the situation in Spain, where many courses have been offered but without substantial reference to the skills needed, and with an excessive emphasis on theoretical matters too remote from the practicalities of real-world job tasks. Training providers are well aware of these deficiencies and some efforts are being put forward to remedy this, such as the so-called "Observatory of occupations" or the reform of vocational training in connection with the general educational reform introduced in 1991 in Spain.

The preceding analysis leads us to conclude that the reform of the state employment offices is an obvious target of future labour market policies. In this sense, the advantages in terms of coordination of having a single agency (the INEM in the case of Spain) managing unemployment insurance, placements and training for the unemployed ought to be weighed against the bureaucratic costs of running together activities which are very different in nature. It is encouraging that both the Government and the social partners agree to this view and talks are already well under way. Two main conclusions seem clear, at any rate: first, the role of INEM as "job broker", to use the OECD terminology (OECD, 1992), should be reinforced, in line with efforts made by some of the regional offices of INEM — the case of Barcelona is outstanding among them; secondly, vocational training courses for the unemployed ought to be provided more in line with market needs and relying more on dual systems which combine theoretical training and actual work practice.

Concluding remarks

In this chapter we have reviewed the evolution over recent years and the current situation of employment policies in Spain. We have emphasized the limited role played so far by "active" labour market measures and the corresponding predominance of income maintenance programmes. Among the "active measures" of employment policy, the promotion of fixed-term contracts has been the main instrument, while employment programmes have played a lesser role. Even more distressing for the efficient operation of the labour market is the lack of efficient employment agencies and training programmes aimed at solving the existing mismatch between labour demand and supply. On the other hand, the unemployment protection system, although providing time-limited benefits and modest replacement ratios, has reduced significantly the personal costs of unemployment. The absence of measures to oblige unemployed people to accept existing job vacancies, and the inability of public employment agencies to help them find such vacancies, constitute the main sources of long-term unemployment.

On the whole, we believe that Spain's labour market does not work as efficiently as it should, which implies that there is room for policies aiming to improve its operation. Among them, we have pinpointed enhancing the placement role of INEM; providing better-focused vocational training courses for the unemployed, with an important practical element; and reforming the unemployment protection system in the sense of clearly separating insurance-based benefits from assistance subsidies. Despite this scope for labour market policies, whose desirability cannot be disputed, we are, however, sceptical about their ability in reducing unemployment. Summing up the argument we have tried to put forward in this book, neither lack of flexibility — in terms of wages or employment — nor labour supply problems are the main reasons for Spain's unemployment. Rather, the weakness of the production structures and the lack of an adequate number of jobs are to blame for it. The Spanish economy needs to grow steadily to provide an adequate job opportunity to the many men and women who want a job and cannot find one. Labour market policies are necessary to make this process smoother and prevent bottlenecks, but cannot be expected to tackle the problem by themselves.

Notes

[1] This table presents data for 1986-89, which corresponds to a period of economic expansion.

[2] Other measures based on wage moderation have also been tried. In this regard, income policies were useful during the first half of the 1980s (see Chapter 4).

[3] In fact, if employers are rational, the effects on hirings should have been small, as we argue in Chapter 4.

[4] In other words, work-sharing does not affect equilibrium unemployment (only, if anything, actual unemployment in the short run) and, therefore, its long-run effects are nil.

[5] These figures are reported by the *Comisión Consultiva Nacional de Convenios Colectivos* [National Consultative Committee on Collective Agreements], annual report, 1990.

[6] The data of this table refer to manufacturing, but the structure of labour costs is very similar across broad sectors (construction, trade, and finance and banking services).

[7] See OECD, 1991, Chapter 7.

[8] For instance, according to the "assistance" principle, there are no reasons to exclude from receipt of unemployment subsidies those unemployed persons without previous work experience and who have not contributed to social security funds.

[9] There are, however, some special exceptions.

[10] In the following description, the post-reform figures will be presented in parentheses.

[11] The existence of a "black economy" (widespread in some regions of Spain), where unemployed people can earn additional income without losing unemployment benefits, is another point to take into account. Thus, if the argument in the text is correct, the elimination of this irregular situation would contribute not only to social justice but also to improving the efficiency of the "legal" labour market.

[12] Ministerio de Trabajo y Seguridad Social: *La política de empleo en España* [Employment policy in Spain], Madrid, 1989.

[13] See, e.g., Calmfors and Nymoen, 1990.

References

Albarracín, F. 1986. "El fundamento empírico de las repercusiones del crecimiento de los salarios sobre el empleo", Madrid, Banco de España, Servicio de Estudios, EC/1986/42.

—; Artola, C. 1989. "El impacto sobre los salarios del cambio ocupacional", in *Economía y Sociología del Trabajo*, No. 6.

Amsden, J. 1972. *Collective bargaining and class conflict in Spain*, London, Weidenfeld and Nicolson.

Andrés, J.; García, J.; Jimenez, S. 1990. "La incidencia y la duración del paro masculino en España", Madrid, Moneda y Crédito.

—; Dolado, J.J.; Molinas, C.; Sebastián, M.; Zabalza, A. 1991. "The influence of demand and capital constraints on Spanish unemployment", in Dréze and Bean, 1991.

Badosa, J. 1979. "La estructura salarial y el funcionamiento del mercado de trabajo en España", in *Información Comercial Española*, No. 553, Sep.

Bean, C.R.; Layard, R.; Nickell, S. (eds.). 1987. *The rise in unemployment*, Oxford, Basil Blackwell.

Bentolila, S.; Bertola, G. 1990. "Firing costs and labour demand: How bad is Eurosclerosis?", in *Review of Economic Studies*, Vol. 57(3), No. 191, pp. 381-402.

—; Blanchard, O. 1990. "Spanish unemployment", in *Economic Policy*, No. 10, pp. 234-281.

—; Dolado, J.J. 1990. "Mismatch and internal migration in Spain, 1962-86", in Padoa Schiopa, 1990.

—; —. 1992. "Who are the insiders? Wage setting in Spanish manufacturing firms", Madrid, Bank of Spain, Working Paper No. 9229 (Servicio de Estudios).

—; Saint-Paul, G. 1992. "The macroeconomic impact of flexible employment contracts: An application to Spain", in *European Economic Review*, No. 36, pp. 1013-1047.

Blanchard, O. 1991. "Unemployment: Getting the questions right and some of the answers", in Dréze and Bean, 1991.

—; Kiyotaki, N. 1987. "Monopolistic competition and the effects of aggregate demand", in *American Economic Review*, Vol. 77, No. 4, pp. 647-666.

—; Summers, L.H. 1986. "Fiscal increasing returns, hysteresis, real wages and unemployment", in *European Economic Review*, Vol. 31, No. 3, pp. 543-560.

Boletín de Estadísticas Laborales. Various issues: Madrid, Ministerio de Trabajo y Seguridad Social.

Bruno, M; Sachs, J. 1985. *Economics of worldwide stagflation*, Oxford, Basil Blackwell.

Burda, M. 1988. "'Wait unemployment' in Europe", in *Economic Policy*, No. 7, pp. 391-425.

Calmfors, L.; Driffill, J. 1988. "Centralization of wage bargaining and macroeconomic performance", in *Economic Policy*, No. 6, pp. 13-61.

—; Nymoen, R. 1990. "Labour market policies and unemployment in the OECD", in *Economic Policy*, No. 11, pp. 449-483.

Cuervo, A. 1986. "La empresa española: Financiación", in *Enciclopedia de la Economía Española*, Vol. 3, pp. 129-144, Barcelona, Editorial Orbis.

Dahrendorf, R., et al. 1986. *Labour market flexibility: Report by a high-level group of experts to the Secretary-General*, Paris, OECD.

De Neubourg, C. 1989. *Unemployment and labour market flexibility: The case of the Netherlands*, Geneva, ILO.

Dolado, J.J. 1991. "Inflación, paro y restricción de oferta en la economía española", in *Boletín Estadístico* (Madrid, Bank of Spain), Dec., pp. 31-34.

—; Malo de Molina, J.L.; Zabalza, A. 1986. "Spanish industrial unemployment: Some explanatory factors", in *Economica*, Vol. 53, No. 210(S), pp. S313-S334.

Donges, J.B. 1984. "La insuficiencia de la productividad en la economía española: Causas y remedios", in J. Linz (ed.): *España: Un presente para el futuro*, Madrid, Instituto de Estudios Económicos.

Drèze, J. 1990. "European unemployment: Lessons from a multi-country study", Université Catholique de Louvain, mimeo.

—; Bean, C.R. (eds.). 1991. *Europe's unemployment problem,* Cambridge, Massachusetts, MIT Press.

Emerson, M. 1988. "Regulation or deregulation of the labour market: Policy regimes for the recruitment and dismissals of employees in the industrialized countries", in *European Economic Review*, Vol. 32, No. 4, pp. 775-817.

Espina, A. 1991. "Un balance de la etapa de implantación de las políticas activas de mercado de trabajo en España: 1983-1989", in S. Bentolila and L. Toharia (eds.): *Estudios de Economia del Trabajo III. El problema del paro*. Ministerio de Trabajo y Seguridad Social, Madrid.

European Commission. 1991. *Employment in Europe*, Brussels.

Fernández, F.J.; Garrido, L.; Toharia, L. 1991. "Empleo y paro en España, 1976-90", in F. Miguélez and C. Prieto (eds.): *Las relaciones laborales en España*, Madrid, Editorial Siglo XXI.

—; Muro, J.; Toharia, L. 1988. *El mercado de trabajo en España en 1987*, Madrid, Fundación IESA.

Fernández Cordón, J. A. 1986. "Análisis longitudinal de la fecundidad en España", Seminario Internacional sobre Tendencias Demográficas y Planificación Económica, Madrid, Ministerio de Economía y Hacienda, May.

Ferner, A. 1988. *Government managers and industrial relations. Public enterprises and their political environment: A comparative study of British Rail and RENFE (Spain)*, Oxford, Basil Blackwell.

Fina, Ll. 1983. "Salaris i fiscalitat. El cas espanyol durant el periode 1965-1975", in *Recerques* (Barcelona), No. 3.

—. 1987. "El paro en España: Sus causas y la respuesta de política económica", in Ll. Fina and L. Toharia: *Las causas del paro en España: Un punto de vista estructural*, Madrid, Fundación IESA.

—; Wilson, R. 1984. "Changes in industrial and occupational employment: An analysis of the Spanish case, 1965-1982", Warwick, Institute for Employment Research, University of Warwick, mimeo.

Freeman, R. 1988. "Labour market institutions and economic performance", in *Economic Policy*, No. 6.

García-Barbancho, A. 1975. *Las migraciones interiores españolas en 1961-70*, Madrid, Instituto de Estudios Económicos.

Gónzalez, L. 1985. "Crisis en la mediana empresa industrial", in *Papeles de Economía Española*, No. 22.

Grubb, D.; Jackman, R.; Layard, R. 1983. "Wage rigidity and unemployment in OECD countries", in *European Economic Review*, Vol. 21, No. 1/2, pp. 11-39.

Instituto Nacional de Estadística. 1992. *La distribución salarial en España*, Madrid.

Jaumandreu, J. 1986. "El empleo en la industria: Destrucción de puestos de trabajo, 1973-82", in *Papeles de Economía Española*, No. 26.

Jimeno, J.F. 1987. "La flexibilidad de los costes laborales nominales en la industria española (1978-82)", in *Investigaciones Económicas*, Vol. XI, No. 3, pp. 483-496.

—. 1991a. "Las estadísticas laborales en España", Madrid, FEDEA, manuscript.

—. 1991b. "The degree of centralization of collective bargaining, the unemployment-inflation trade-offs and microeconomic efficiency revisited", Madrid, FEDEA, mimeo.

—. 1992. "Las implicaciones macroeconómicas de la negociación colectiva: El caso español", in *Móneda y Crédito*, No. 195 (forthcoming).

—; Meixide, A. 1991. "Collective bargaining and wage dynamics in Spain", Madrid, FEDEA, mimeo.

—; Toharia, L. 1991a. "Spanish labour markets: Institutions and outcomes", Paper presented to the International Workshop on Comparative Labour Market Institutions and Contracts, Wassenaar, Netherlands, Jan. 1991.

—; —. 1991b. "The productivity and wage effects of fixed-term contracts: Empirical evidence from Spain", Paper presented to the Third Conference of the European Association of Labour Economists, El Escorial, Spain, Aug. 1991.

—; —. 1991c. "The productivity effects of fixed-term employment contracts: Are temporary workers less productive than permanent workers?", Universidad de Alcalá de Henares, mimeo.

Labour Force Survey [Encuesta de Población Activa]. Various years. Madrid, Instituto Nacional de Estadística.

Lamo, A.R.; Dolado, J.J. 1991. "Un modelo del mercado de trabajo y la restricción de oferta en la economía española", Bank of Spain, Working Paper No. 9116.

Layard, R.; Bean, C.R. 1990. "Why does unemployment persist?", in S. Honkapohja (ed.): *The state of macroeconomics*, Oxford, Basil Blackwell.

—; Jackman; R.; Savouri, S. 1990. "Mismatch: A framework for thought", in F. Padoa Schioppa, 1991.

—; Nickell, S. 1986. "Unemployment in Britain", in *Economica*, Vol. 53, No. 210(S), pp. 121-170.

—; —; Jackman, R. 1991. *Unemployment*, Oxford, Oxford University Press.

Lindbeck, A.; Snower, D.J. 1988. The insider-outsider theory, Cambridge, Massachussetts, MIT Press.

Lorente, J.R. 1982. "Notas críticas sobre las estadísticas salariales españolas", in A. Espina, Ll. Fina and J.R. Lorente (eds.): *El mercado de trabajo en España*, Madrid, Ministerio de Trabajo y Seguridad Social.

—. 1986. "Una nota sobre los factores explicativos de la demanda de trabajo", in *Boletín de Información Comercial Española*, No. 2041.

—. 1987. "La inestabilidad muestral de la Encuesta de Salarios", in *Boletín de Información Comercial Española*, No. 2068.

Malo de Molina, J.L. 1984. "Distorsión y ajuste del mercado de trabajo español", in *Papeles de Economía Española*, No. 21, pp. 214-235.

—. 1985. "Coherencia del sistema de relaciones industriales y eficiencia del mercado de trabajo", in *Papeles de Economía Española*, No. 22, pp. 244-264.

— (ed.). 1988. *El debate sobre la flexibilidad del mercado de trabajo*, Madrid, Fundación para la Investigación Económica y Social (FIES).

—; Ortega, E. 1984. "El excedente bruto de explotación en la industria española: Aproximaciones a la tasa de rentabilidad", in *Boletín Económico del Banco de España*, Dec.

Martín, C.; Rodriguez, L. 1977. *Cambio técnico y dependencia tecnológica*, Madrid, Fundación del INI.

Martinez, J.A., et al. 1982. *Economía Española*: 1960-1980, Madrid, H. Blume Ediciones.

Miguelez, F. 1977. *SEAT. La empresa modelo del régimen*, Barcelona, Dopesa.

Ministerio de Economía. Various years. *La negociación colectiva en las grandes empresas*, Madrid.

Ministerio de Trabajo y Seguridad Social. 1985. *Analísis económico-financiero de la Seguridad Social*, Madrid.

—. 1989. *La política de empleo en España*, Madrid.

Molero, J. 1983. *Tecnologia e industrialización*, Madrid, Ed. Pirámide.

OECD. 1986a. *Education and training for manpower development*, Paris.

—. 1986b. *Employment Outlook*, Paris.

—. 1991. *Employment Outlook*, Paris.

—. Various years. *Historical statistics*, Paris.

Padoa Schioppa, F. (ed.). 1990. *Mismatch and labour mobility*, London, Centre for Economic Policy Research (CEPR).

Saint-Paul, G. 1990. "The high unemployment trap", Cambridge, Massachussetts, MIT Press, mimeo.

Salter, W. 1966. *Productivity and technical change*, Cambridge, United Kingdom, Cambridge University Press.

Segura, J. 1983. "La crisis económica como crisis industrial: La necesidad de una estrategia activa", in *Papeles de Economía Española*, No. 15.

—; Jamandreu, J. 1987. "Algunos resultados sobre la importancia del cambio técnico en la industria española", in *Cuadernos Económicos del ICE*, No. 37, pp. 71-79.

—; Durán, F.; Toharia L.; Bentolila, S. 1991. *Análisis de la contratación temporal en España*, Madrid, Ministerio de Trabajo y Seguridad Social.

Serrano, A.; Malo de Molina, J.L. 1978. *Salario y mercado de trabajo en España*, Madrid, H. Blume Ediciones.

Solow, R. 1986. "Unemployment: Getting the questions right", in *Economica*, Vol. 53, No. 210(S).

Standing, G. 1989. *Unemployment and labour market flexibility: The United Kingdom*, Geneva, ILO.

Toharia, L. 1981. "Precios, costes, beneficios y la 'Tasa justificada de inflación' en la economía española, 1965-1979", in *Investigaciones Económicas*, No. 16.

—. 1985a. "La flexibilización del mercado de trabajo: Algunas reflexiones teóricas", in *Reparto de Trabajo e Integración Social de los Jóvenes*, Madrid, Editorial Siglo XXI.

—. 1985b. "En torno a la supuesta rigidez del mercado de trabajo en España", in *Círculo de Empresarios*, second quarter, pp. 47-63.

—. 1986. "Un fordisme inachevé, entre transition politique et crise économique: Espagne", in R. Boyer: *La flexibilité du travail en Europe*, Paris, La Découverte (English translation published as R. Boyer: *The search for labour market flexibility*, Oxford, Oxford University Press, 1988.

—. 1987. "Salarios y beneficios: El caso de la economia española (1965-85)", in *Revista del Treball*, Mar. pp. 79-91.

—. 1988. "La flexibilidad del mercado de trabajo en España: ¿Positiva o negativa?", in Malo de Molina (ed.), 1988.

—. 1991. "El paro femenino en España: Algunos elementos para el análisis", in *Revista de Economía y Sociología del Trabajo*, No. 13-14.

Viñals, J. 1983. "El mercado de trabajo y sus implicaciones para las políticas macroeconómicas de ajuste: El caso de España", in *Papeles de Economía Española*, No. 15, pp. 258-275 (reprinted in S. Bentolila and L. Toharia, 1991, *Estudios de economía del trabajo en España, III. El problema del paro*, Madrid, Ministerio de Trabajo y Seguridad Social).

Appendix

Logit models of the probability of escaping unemployment into employment between 1988 and 1990, by gender

	Females				Males			
	Coefficient	t	Probability	Difference of probability	Coefficient	t	Probability	Difference of probability
CONSTANT	−0.357	−1.44	41.2		0.679	4.15	66.3	
OTHER UNEMP.	−0.771	−8.52	24.4	−16.7	−0.431	−6.32	56.2	−10.2
OTHER EMP.	0.244	2.26	47.2	6.0	−0.073	−1.01	64.7	−1.7
16-19	0.326	3.23	49.2	8.0	−0.141	−1.31	63.1	−3.2
25-29	−0.143	−1.61	37.7	−3.4	0.002	0.02	66.4	0.0
30-34	−0.336	−2.84	33.3	−7.8	−0.381	−3.31	57.4	−9.0
35-39	−0.479	−3.37	30.2	−10.9	−0.566	−4.11	52.8	−13.5
40-49	−0.832	−5.44	23.3	−17.8	−0.903	−6.92	44.4	−21.9
50 &>	−1.152	−5.16	18.1	−23.1	−1.540	−11.20	29.7	−36.6
NO HH EMPD.	0.148	−0.66	37.6	−3.5	0.186	1.31	70.4	4.0
NO HH UNEMP.	0.475	1.90	52.9	11.8	0.007	0.04	66.5	0.2
NO HH INACTIVE.	−0.175	−0.80	37.0	−4.2	−0.204	−1.59	61.6	−4.7
MARRIED	−0.441	−4.81	31.0	−10.1	0.529	4.26	77.0	10.6
OTHER	0.143	0.74	44.7	3.5	0.099	0.44	68.5	2.2
NO EDUCN.	0.280	1.78	48.1	6.9	0.321	3.34	73.1	6.8
LOW SEC. EDUCN.	−0.113	−1.29	38.5	−2.7	0.046	0.59	67.4	1.0
SECONDARY	−0.096	−0.80	38.8	−2.3	−0.179	−1.50	62.2	−4.1
VOC.TR.	0.115	1.05	44.0	2.8	0.174	1.55	70.1	3.8
UNIVERSITY	0.689	6.16	58.2	17.1	0.136	0.95	69.3	3.0
STUDY	−1.503	−13.24	13.5	−27.7	−2.025	−13.62	20.7	−45.7
FSIZE1	−0.073	−0.18	39.4	−1.7	−0.528	−1.85	53.8	−12.6
FSIZE2	0.043	0.34	42.2	1.0	−0.411	−3.46	56.7	−9.7
FSIZE3	−0.168	−1.82	37.2	−4.0	−0.331	−3.76	58.6	−7.7
FSIZE5	0.165	1.83	45.2	4.1	−0.123	−1.45	63.5	−2.8
FSIZE6	0.099	0.90	43.6	2.4	0.168	1.64	70.0	3.7
FSIZE>6	0.189	1.60	45.8	4.6	−0.168	−1.66	62.5	−3.8

Log-Likelihood	-3164.3	Log-Likelihood	-3563.8
Restricted (Slopes=0) Log-L	-3409.0	Restricted (Slopes=0) Log-L	-3864.3
Chi-Squared (25)	489.57	Chi-Squared (25)	601.00
Significance Level	-32173E-13	Significance Level	-32173E-13

Characteristics of the reference individual:
— there is no other unemployed in the household;
— there is no other employed in the household;
— age: 20-24 years;
— household head;
— single;
— primary education;
— is not currently studying;
— family size: 4.

Explanation of variables:
— CONSTANT: reference individual;
— OTHER UNEMP.: another household member is unemployed;
— OTHER EMP.: another household member is employed;

— 16-19, 25-29,...:age groups (self-explanatory);
— NO HH EMPD.: not household head (HH) and the HH is employed;
— NO HH UNEMP.: not household head (HH) and the HH is unemployed;
— NO HH INACTIVE: not household head (HH) and the HH is out of the labour force (inactive);
— MARRIED: married;
— OTHER: neither single nor married;
— NO EDUCN.: is illiterate or with no formal education;
— LOW SEC. EDUCN: lower secondary education (equivalent to 8 years of education);
— SECONDARY: higher secondary education (11 years); VOC.TR.: some vocational training degree; UNIVERSITY: university degree (either 3 or 5 years);
— STUDY: undertaking some form of regular education in reference week.